Weight Shift

Weight Shift

Navigating Your First Few Steps of Faith in Jesus

BRANDON BERG

Forewords by A. J. Swoboda
& Chris Hansler

WIPF & STOCK · Eugene, Oregon

WEIGHT SHIFT
Navigating Your First Few Steps of Faith in Jesus

Copyright © 2025 Brandon Berg. All rights reserved. Except for brief quotations in critical publications or reviews, no part of this book may be reproduced in any manner without prior written permission from the publisher. Write: Permissions, Wipf and Stock Publishers, 199 W. 8th Ave., Suite 3, Eugene, OR 97401.

Wipf & Stock
An Imprint of Wipf and Stock Publishers
199 W. 8th Ave., Suite 3
Eugene, OR 97401

www.wipfandstock.com

PAPERBACK ISBN: 979-8-3852-4914-5
HARDCOVER ISBN: 979-8-3852-4915-2
EBOOK ISBN: 979-8-3852-4916-9

VERSION NUMBER 08/21/25

Scripture quotations marked (CEB) from the COMMON ENGLISH BIBLE. © Copyright 2011 COMMON ENGLISH BIBLE. All rights reserved. Used by permission. (www.CommonEnglishBible.com)

Scripture quotations marked (AMP) are taken from the AMPLIFIED® BIBLE, Copyright© 1954, 1958, 1962, 1964, 1965, 1987 by the Lockman Foundation Used by Permission. (www.Lockman.org)

Scripture quotations marked (NKJV) are taken from the NEW KING JAMES VERSION®. Copyright© 1982 by Thomas Nelson, Inc. Used by permission. All rights reserved.

Scripture quotations marked (NLT) are taken from the Holy Bible, New Living Translation, copyright ©1996, 2004, 2015 by Tyndale House Foundation. Used by permission of Tyndale House Publishers, Carol Stream, Illinois 60188. All rights reserved.

Scripture marked (GNT) taken from the Good News Translation—Second Edition, Copyright 1992 by American Bible Society. Used by Permission.

Scripture marked (ESV) are from The ESV® Bible (The Holy Bible, English Standard Version®), © 2001 by Crossway, a publishing ministry of Good News Publishers. Used by permission. All rights reserved.

Scripture marked (NIV) taken from The Holy Bible, New International Version®, NIV®. Copyright © 1973, 1978, 1984, 2011 by Biblica, Inc. Used with permission of Zondervan. All rights reserved worldwide. www.zondervan.com

Scripture quotations marked (MSG) are taken from THE MESSAGE, copyright © 1993, 2002, 2018 by Eugene H. Peterson. Used by permission of NavPress, represented by Tyndale House Publishers. All rights reserved.

To Joy: thank you for getting in the wheelbarrow while I often stood on the edge of faith.

To my kids: I love you, and I pray real, simple, consistent prayers for you.

To my grandkids: may you shift your weight in the direction of Jesus all your days.

Contents

Foreword by A. J. Swoboda | *ix*

Foreword by Chris Hansler | *xi*

Acknowledgments | *xiii*

Abbreviations | *xiv*

Introduction | *xvii*

1. The Best News Ever: The Gospel | 1
2. Introducing Jesus, God, and the Holy Spirit . . . or Just God | 10
3. Introducing the Bible | 33
4. Introducing Faith: Belief vs. Trust | 49
5. Introducing the Goal: Look in the Mirror | 52
6. Introducing Some Potential Next Steps | 55

   Conclusion | 88

Appendix | *89*

Bibliography | *91*

Foreword by A. J. Swoboda

My mom always told me about the memories she couldn't shake from her childhood—the assassination of John F. Kennedy Jr., how her dad kindly reacted when she crashed her first car, how her grandmother always had a bowl of candy at the ready whenever they'd play cards together. Odd, isn't it, the things we remember? The memory is picky. She once recounted watching the television as the first human beings took a step upon the moon. The moment is transfixed in all of our minds. As Neil Armstrong, the first human to step on the giant ball of space dust we call the moon, he spoke, simply, "That's one small step for man, one giant leap for mankind."

The book in your hands is an invitation to take your first few steps. My friend, Brandon Berg, is a man who takes seriously the journey to starting a relationship with Jesus. He wrote this book for you—for those who are beginning to take their first small steps of faith. It may seem like these steps are simple and unimportant—just like taking a step on the moon may not seem like a big deal. But it is not the step that is important. It is the journey you've chosen that is important. A step on earth is no big deal. But a step in the kingdom of God is everything.

Some of these first steps may seem easy. This includes things like learning to go to church, or praying before a meal, or being kinder to your coworkers. But other steps will feel very challenging: learning to be generous, forgiving someone who deeply

Foreword by A. J. Swoboda

harmed or hurt you, repenting of sins or addictions that have controlled us, and choosing to see God as the center of the universe rather than yourselves. Just because some seem easy and some seem hard, you are assured—not by me but by the powerful words of Scripture—that God has given you the Holy Spirit to walk these steps faithfully. You have been given the "deposit" (2 Cor 1:22) of the Holy Spirit because you have decided to follow Jesus. Now that you have the Spirit in your life, you are to begin to walk. As Paul would say: "I say, then, walk in the Spirit" (Gal 5:25).

Learning to walk is no small thing. Some, out of fear, never risk taking their first step. It feels too daunting, scary, embarrassing, lonely, novel. But keep in mind that every single Olympian has one thing in common: they all had a first step. Put aside any of that fear, trepidation, and concern and trust the words of Brandon. He is reaching out his hand. And he wants to see you learn to walk.

Even as I write this, I pray to God on your behalf. God is with you. The journey will challenge you, push you, frustrate you. But it is a journey that will lead to the presence of God in the here and the future. Remain faithful. And you will never have regrets.

A. J. Swoboda, PhD
Lent 2025
Eugene, Oregon

Foreword by Chris Hansler

FAITH CAN BE INTIMIDATING, especially at the beginning. For the person who has just whispered a hesitant prayer, attended their first church service, or cracked open the Bible for the very first time, the journey ahead can feel at the same time exciting and overwhelming. That's what makes *Weight Shift* so needed—and so timely.

In a world where spiritual language can often be complex and Christian literature assumes familiarity, this book stands apart. Brandon does not fill this book with dense jargon or lofty assumptions. Instead, *Weight Shift* is a warm, clear, and genuinely accessible companion for the earliest steps of faith. Whether you're standing at the edge of belief or have just taken your first few steps into following Jesus, this book meets you right where you are.

What strikes me is the readability of this guide. Using helpful illustrations and meaningful stories, Brandon has written with the heart of a pastor and the clarity of a mentor, breaking down foundational truths into language that anyone can understand. Complex theological ideas are explained with grace and simplicity, without ever compromising the depth of their meaning. From understanding who Jesus is to learning how to pray, read the Bible, and engage in community, each chapter builds on the last like a conversation with a trusted friend.

Most importantly, *Weight Shift* doesn't just offer helpful information; it grounds everything in the central truths of the Christian

Foreword by Chris Hansler

faith: the gospel of Jesus Christ, the character of God, the invitation to follow, and the promise of transformation. These are not ideas to merely believe, but truths to build a life upon. The tone is kind but confident, compassionate yet anchored in Scripture, offering a wide welcome to the spiritually curious while pointing to the narrow way that leads to life.

If you've recently begun your faith journey—or are walking alongside someone who has—this book is a gift. And more than that, it's a tool: to help steady your footing, clarify your questions, and encourage your next step.

    Christ Hansler,
    Regional Executive Director,
    Open Bible Churches

Acknowledgments

Linda Scheele, thank you for your generosity in editing the initial manuscript.

Jess Hardy, I'm grateful for your generosity and legal mind.

Abbreviations

Abbreviations for books of the bible used in *Weight Shift*

OLD TESTAMENT (OT)

Book	Abbreviation
Genesis	Gen
Exodus	Exod
Judges	Judg
1 Kings	1 Kgs
Job	Job
Proverbs	Prov
Isaiah	Isa
Daniel	Dan
Malachi	Mal

NEW TESTAMENT (NT)

Book	Abbreviation
Matthew	Matt
Mark	Mark
Luke	Luke
John	John
Acts	Acts

Abbreviations

Book	Abbreviation
Romans	Rom
1 Corinthians	1 Cor
Galatians	Gal
Ephesians	Eph
Philippians	Phil
1 Thessalonians	1 Thess
Hebrews	Heb
James	Jas
1 John	1 John
Jude	Jude
Revelation	Rev

Introduction

AT 7:05 A.M. ON August 7, 1974, after six years in the making, high-wire artist Philippe Petit took his first step onto a cable roughly one inch in diameter, suspended roughly 1,350 feet above street level. The wire was about 200 feet long and stretched between the 110-story Twin Towers in New York.

His walk lasted about fifty minutes, where he crossed back and forth about eight times, sat down at one point, and even laid down on the wire once. At about 7:55 a.m., he finally surrendered himself (yes, you guessed it) to the NYPD. Apparently, stringing cables between high-rise buildings in New York City and attempting to walk across them might get you in trouble with the authorities. Go figure.

Talking later about his experience in a TED Talk in March of 2012, he said this:

> On top of the World Trade Center, my first step was ... terrifying. All of a sudden, the density of the air is no longer the same. Manhattan no longer spreads its infinity; the murmur of the city dissolves into a squall whose chill and power I no longer feel. . . . I lift the balancing pole, I approach the edge, I step over the beam. I put my left foot on the cable. The weight of my body rests on my right leg, anchored to the flank of the building. Shall I ever so slightly shift my weight to the left, my right leg will be unburdened, my right foot will freely meet the wire. . . . An inner howl assails me: the wild longing to

Introduction

flee. But it is too late. The wire is ready. Decisively, my other foot sets itself onto the cable.[1]

This book has likely landed in your hands because you have recently "shifted your weight" from your back foot of doubt or unbelief toward your front foot of faith. I use the word "toward" purposefully. For some, yes, your weight is now fully shifted. But for others, the shift from doubt to faith, unbelief to belief, is somewhere in between your back foot and front foot. You are in process, on a journey, not arrived. More on this later.

This Little Book's Origin Story

This book was born out of need in the middle of a Bible study on the book of James. Like many churches, a lot of our people meet in small groups of 8–10 people to study the Bible and build relational connections. A lady in one of our small groups quit after one week and sent this message to the group: "I'm not going to be able to make it. I appreciated the community and listening to everyone's insights, but I think this study is too advanced for my faith." After some conversation via email with our struggling faith sojourner, I received an email from the group leader. She wanted to know if I knew of a study or book she could walk through with this person in a one-on-one basis to help her take another small step along the faith journey. I was stumped. I contacted pastors, Bible teachers, various church leaders, seminary professors, and multiple theologians to ask if they were aware of a basic (*very* basic) introduction to the Christian faith. In return, I received blank stares, long pauses, and a hodgepodge list of recommendations. I found it telling that one such list came from a well-known theologian friend of mine via Zoom as he sat in his office with a wall of books as his backdrop, no doubt many of them works of theology and none he could point to that would offer a basic introduction to the Christian faith. Imagine, after two thousand years of church history, I

---

1. Petit, "Philippe Petit," 08:07–09:45.

Introduction

Regardless, if any of these potential scenarios describes you—this book is for you.

A Note to Pastors and Ministry Leaders

You are a hero to me. At the time of this writing, I've spent about twenty-seven years in full-time ministry as a staff pastor, church planter, and lead pastor. I know the pressures you face and the things that keep you up at night. My pastor used to tell me, "Pastoring on a good day is hard enough." Finances, administration, board meetings, other meetings, managing conflict, ever-changing culture, staff development, personal development, vision casting, worship service planning, weddings, funerals, pastoral counseling, and . . . oh yeah, carving out time for study and preparing for the weekly spiritual diet of the local church or ministry where you've been called.

Above all this is your love for Jesus, the gospel, the church, and changed lives. There is something that stirs in you every time someone places their faith in Jesus and is baptized into the family of God. It never gets old.

A central goal in crafting this book is to honor as many theological streams within the Christian faith as possible. So, my prayer is this work will be a blessing to you and those coming to faith under your care. Where I sensed there is ongoing in-house debate regarding a particular subject, I did my best to turn the reader's heart back to you, their pastor, and the local church.

How to Read This Book

If you received this book from a friend and they are willing to go through it with you, I encourage you to take them up on the offer. If you find yourself alone with the book, don't worry—this book was designed for the solo traveler in mind too.

Likely, somewhere in your community is a beautiful, imperfect, Jesus-loving church led by a pastor(s) and team of people who

Introduction

have given their lives to helping people grow in their faith. At some point, it's going to be in your best interest to connect with that church if you haven't already, especially if you're reading this book on your own. They will be a resource to help answer questions and help you shift your weight toward your next step of faith.

One last note before we begin: philosopher, poet, and novelist George Santayana is often attributed with the saying, "There are books in which the footnotes, or the comments scrawled by some reader's hand in the margin, are more interesting than the text." I encourage you to pay close attention to the footnotes throughout the book; I think you'll find them to be a source of clarity along your journey.

1

The Best News Ever
The Gospel

"The gospel has been described as a pool in which a toddler can wade and yet an elephant can swim. It is both simple enough to tell to a child and profound enough for the greatest minds to explore."[1]

GOSPEL MUSIC. THE "GOSPEL TRUTH." Preach the gospel. A gospel choir. A gospel church. What does this word "gospel" mean?

At its core, the word means to declare something as good news. Still, what is the good news the Christian faith refers to, and more specifically, what is the good news of Jesus Christ? What does the Bible mean when it uses this word?

New Testament[2] theologian Scot McKnight defines the gospel of Jesus Christ in part this way: "The gospel is to announce good news about key events in the life of Jesus Christ."[3]

---

1. Keller, "Gospel."
2. The books of Matthew to Revelation in the Bible, sometimes referred to as the Greek Scriptures since they are mostly written in Greek in the original text.
3. McKnight, *King Jesus Gospel*, 50.

What are those key events, you might ask? Good question. McKnight spends considerable time unpacking 1 Cor 15 and outlines some of the following in his book as key ingredients to the gospel of Jesus Christ. Obviously, I've left out much of what he has to say, and combined a few of his "Key Events" for brevity.

Key Event #1: Jesus Fulfills the Old Testament[4] Scriptures

> "I passed on to you as most important what I also received: Christ died for our sins in line with the Scriptures."—1 Corinthians 15:3, CEB

As you become familiar with the Old Testament portion of the Bible, you will notice anticipation building for a Savior. A yearning for a Messiah.[5] What stokes this anticipation in God's people is prophesy[6] about the coming Messiah, and much of it was remarkably detailed.

In his book *Evidence that Demands a Verdict*, author Josh McDowell states there are about 333 Old Testament Prophecies detailing who the coming Messiah would be. Seventy of these Prophecies are primary, and the other 263 are secondary, or what McDowell calls "ramifications" of the seventy primary Prophecies. These Prophecies were uttered hundreds of years before Jesus was born and contained such detail as the Messiah's exact lineage, location of his birth, and even the manner of his death by Roman

---

4. The books of Genesis to Malachi in the Bible, sometimes referred to as the Hebrew Scriptures since they are mostly written in Hebrew in the original text.

5. "The promised deliverer of the Jewish nation and redeemer of the human race prophesied in the Hebrew Scriptures; (*Christian Church*) Jesus Christ regarded as the fulfilment of this promise." Oxford English Dictionary, "Messiah" (italics original).

6. "To speak or write by, or as by, divine inspiration, or in the name of God or a god; to speak or act as a prophet." Oxford English Dictionary, "Prophesy." Author's note: The use here is regarding Old Testament prophets and their prophesy. However, there is a spiritual gift of prophesy outlined in the New Testament that differs in some ways from the function of the Old Testament prophet. I encourage you to talk with your pastor about this distinction.

crucifixion—which, by the way, wasn't even introduced into the Roman capital punishment system until hundreds of years after the biblical prophecy was given![7]

What are the odds that one person could fulfill all seventy major Old Testament messianic Prophecies? The number is incalculable. Let's consider someone fulfilling just eight of them. The mathematical probability is 10^{17}. That is a ten with seventeen zeros behind it! McDowell illustrates the magnitude of this number by suggesting his reader imagine the entire state of Texas piled two feet high with silver dollars. Now, imagine picking one up and placing a red "x" on it, throwing it back in the sea of silver dollars, mixing the whole thing up, then blindfolding yourself only to walk the length and breadth of the great state of Texas. You then stop at random, thrust your hand in the pile and pull out that exact silver dollar with the red "x" on it. Impossible. Here's the kicker—Jesus fulfilled all seventy primary Prophecies, and all 263 secondary ones too![8]

KEY EVENT #2: THE INCARNATION[9] OF JESUS (GOD IN A BOD!)

"The Word became flesh and made his home among us."
(John 1:14, CEB)

On Christmas Eve of 1854, the world-renowned pastor and preacher, Charles Spurgeon, preached a sermon entitled "The Birth of Christ" wherein he expounds on one of God's names: *Immanuel*, which means "God with us." Woven throughout his sermon are expressions of awe and wonder at the seemingly incomprehensible

---

7. McDowell, *Evidence*, 277–333.
8. McDowell and McDowell, *Evidence*, 409–11.
9. "The action of incarnating or fact of being incarnated or 'made flesh'; a becoming incarnate; investiture or embodiment in flesh; assumption of, or existence in, a bodily (esp. human) form." Oxford English Dictionary, "Incarnation."

idea of God becoming a human being. Why would God do this? And why is it important for me?

Here is an excerpt from his sermon:

> Oh! may God teach you the meaning of that name Immanuel, "God with us"! . . . "Immanuel." It is wisdom's mystery, "God with us." Sages look at it, and wonder; angels desire to see it; the plumb-line of reason cannot reach half-way into its depths. . . . "God with us." . . . Ah! and to finish, "God with us,"—'tis eternity's sonnet, 'tis heaven's hallelujah, 'tis the shout of the glorified, 'tis the song of the redeemed, 'tis the chorus of angels, 'tis the everlasting oratorio of the great orchestra of the sky. "God with us."[10]

'Tis good stuff. No other religion in the world boasts about their god becoming human. Only Christianity makes this claim. Immanuel, God with us.

Imagine one of the most difficult seasons of your life. Now consider some of the things that brought you the most encouragement. Let me venture a guess—one element of encouragement you experienced is when you encountered someone who had experienced the same pain. They heard your story, and you heard theirs, and noticed they had "walked in your shoes." Perhaps the feeling of loneliness dissipated a little because they could relate to you, and you could relate to them. You were no longer alone. You had shared experience.

C. S. Lewis, the famed creator of *The Chronicles of Narnia*, wrote a book entitled *The Four Loves* where he explores the various types of love outlined in Scripture. When talking about the love that accompanies friendship he makes this beautiful statement: "Friendship . . . is born at the moment when one man says to another, 'What! You too? I thought that no one but myself.'"[11]

About 750 years before Jesus was born, one of Israel's most famous prophets described portions of Jesus's life this way:

---

10. Spurgeon, "Birth of Christ."
11. Lewis, *Four Loves*, 100.

> He was despised and avoided by others; / a man who suffered, who knew sickness well. / Like someone from whom people hid their faces, / he was despised, and we didn't think about him. / It was certainly our sickness that he carried, / and our sufferings that he bore, / but we thought him afflicted, / struck down by God and tormented. / He was pierced because of our rebellions / and crushed because of our crimes. / He bore the punishment that made us whole; / by his wounds we are healed.[12]

Similarly, the writer of Heb 4:14 tells us that Jesus can sympathize with our weakness because he was human and tempted in every way we are tempted.

My prayer is that as you experience Jesus, you will find your heart declaring these words to him: "What! You too? I thought no one but myself . . ." You have a friend. He's walked in your shoes and continues to walk with you today through the person of the Holy Spirit (more on this later). You're not alone!

KEY EVENT #3: THE DEATH OF JESUS

> "I passed on to you as most important what I also received: Christ died for our sins in line with the Scriptures." —1 Corinthians 15:3, CEB

> "I have tried to explain what Jesus has done for us when he died. I've done so by distilling some principles. I can't do the doctrine of the Cross full justice, however."[13]

Millions of people around the world make and wear cross-shaped jewelry. In fact, I just completed a Google search for "cross jewelry" and received 122,000,000 results in .48 seconds. I wonder if you've ever considered that the cross is an instrument of death and humiliation? Doesn't it seem odd to you that jewelers would use an expensive, precious metal and spend their valuable time and well-developed skill to craft a symbol of torture? Further, who would willingly pay hard-earned money to prominently display a

---

12. Isa 53:3–5 (CEB).
13. Keller, *Reason for God*, 205.

symbol of torture and death? Seems a little dark, no? OK, I wear a cross necklace. Still, it's a little strange isn't it?

History reveals to us that the Assyrians, Babylonians, and Persians used crucifixion long before it was introduced into Roman culture. The Romans reserved it for slaves, criminals, non-citizens, and Christians. Rarely, if ever, would it be used as a means of death for a Roman citizen, mainly because the process was so humiliating and excruciating. They spent five hundred years perfecting it before it was outlawed by Constantine in the fourth century.

The process generally went something like this: a prisoner convicted and sentenced to death often would be stripped, beaten, and then whipped with a flagrum.[14] Again, the Romans spent hundreds of years perfecting the "art" of crucifixion and the Roman soldiers knew how to manipulate the flagrum for maximum impact. The result was not just a few bloody stripes, rather a back (and other body parts) reduced to open, raw flesh as the recipient's skin was peeled away by the bone and metal shards embedded in the whip.

If the convicted criminal was unlucky enough to survive this initial scourging, they would often be forced to carry a portion of the wood they would soon be nailed to upon reaching the crucifixion site. The convict was then stretched out on the cross and large four-to-five-inch iron stakes were used to pin the body to the wood. A hole was dug and the end of the cross was then dropped into the hole, sending jarring shock waves of pain through the victim's body. Once suspended, the prisoner would suffer a long, slow, excruciating death (hours to even days), ultimately succumbing to either asphyxiation, dehydration, or heart failure. In fact, because the lungs would begin to fill with fluid, prisoners were known to push upward off the nail(s) in their feet to help themselves breathe. To combat this, the Romans were known to break the legs of the victims, or pierce their side with a spear in an effort to hasten death.

---

14. Often a leather braided whip with metal balls, and/or pieces of bone and metal embedded in the leather.

The Best News Ever

So, we know crucifixion is an unfortunate historical fact of human history. But, is it a historical fact that Jesus was crucified?

Certainly the Bible makes clear that he was. All four Gospel writers—Matthew, Mark, Luke, and John—detail the crucifixion of Christ. But is there historical evidence outside the Bible?

A first-century, non-Christian, Jewish historian named Flavius Josephus wrote a book entitled *The Antiquities of the Jews*. In it, he noted this about Jesus:

> Now there was about this time Jesus, a wise man, if it be lawful to call him a man; for he was a doer of wonderful works, a teacher of such men as receive the truth with pleasure. He drew over to him both many of the Jews and many of the Gentiles. He was [the] Christ. And when Pilate, at the suggestion of the principal men amongst us, had condemned him to the cross, those that loved him at the first did not forsake him; for he appeared to them alive again the third day; as the divine prophets had foretold these and ten thousand other wonderful things concerning him. And the tribe of Christians, so named from him, are not extinct at this day.[15]

Here's another quote by a Roman historian and politician, a man named Tacitus:

> Therefore, to scotch the rumour, Nero substituted as culprits, and punished with the utmost refinements of cruelty, a class of men, loathed for their vices, whom the crowd styled Christians. Christus, the founder of the name, had undergone the death penalty in the reign of Tiberius, by sentence of the procurator Pontius Pilatus.[16]

Both the Bible and ancient secular historians affirm that Jesus was crucified. At the core of the gospel—the good news—is the reality that he took your place and my place on the cross.

But, that's not the end of the story.

---

15. Josephus, *Antiquities of the Jews* 18.3.
16. Tacitus, *Annals of Tacitus* 15.44.

Weight Shift

Key Event #4: The Resurrection of Jesus, and His Appearances to Others

> "I passed on to you as most important what I also received: Christ died for our sins in line with the Scriptures, he was buried, and he rose on the third day.... And then he appeared to more than five hundred brothers and sisters at once." —1 Corinthians 15:3–4, 6 CEB

> "If Jesus rose from the dead, then you have to accept all that he said; if he didn't rise from the dead, then why worry about any of what he said? The issue on which everything hangs is not whether or not you like his teaching but whether or not he rose from the dead." —Timothy Keller[17]

The resurrection of Jesus Christ is the pivot point in all human history, and the lynchpin of all Christian faith and thought. Anyone who claims to be God—which Jesus did repeatedly (John 5:39–40; 8:56–59; 10:30–33; Luke 5:20–25)—predicts their own death and resurrection, and then pulls it off . . . well, we have a really important decision to make about such a person.

In fact, let me ask you a question: what would it take for your sibling to convince you they were God? Exactly—you'd be on the phone to the nearest psychiatric intake clinic. It was the same with Jesus. He had brothers and sisters (Mark 6:3), and none of them believed in his divinity during his entire earthly ministry. Yet today we have an ancient letter preserved in the Bible called James that was written by Jesus' half-brother. What could possibly move James from ardent disbelief in his brother Jesus as the Messiah to a wholehearted belief that Jesus was indeed God? One thing: the resurrection. In fact, James' belief was so devoted that he was willing to die for it, which history tells us he did.

The Bible tells us Jesus was resurrected three days after being crucified (Matt 28; Mark 16; Luke 24; John 20), then walked the earth for forty days (Acts 1:1–3), and appeared to more than five hundred people during this time (1 Cor 15:6).

I can hear the objections already: "Well, is it only the Bible that confirms Jesus' resurrection? That's not super convincing." Let's go

---

17. Keller, *Reason for God*, 210.

back to our non-Christian Jewish historian Josephus. Remember, as a non-Christian there is no benefit for him to write this. None. He was simply doing his work as a historian to accurately record what was happening:

> He was [the] Christ; and when Pilate, at the suggestion of the principal men amongst us, had condemned him to the cross, those that loved him at the first did not forsake him, for he appeared to them alive again the third day, as the divine prophets had foretold these and ten thousand other wonderful things.[18]

Christianity is the only world religion that boasts a resurrected leader; all other world religions can visit the grave where their leader is entombed.

Jesus rose from the dead, punctuating all he taught, the miracles he performed, and all he claimed to be. Jesus ... is ... alive!

The gospel: Jesus is the Messiah prophesied in the Old Testament, he came in the flesh, he died and rose again!

CHAPTER 1 DISCUSSION QUESTIONS:

1. What part of the story of Jesus (the gospel) captures your heart the most?

2. How was the gospel first shared with you?

3. What comes to your mind when you think about God becoming a human (the incarnation of Christ)?

4. Can you think of someone you would want to share the gospel with? What is one way you could do this?

---

18. Josephus, *Antiquities of the Jews* 18.3.

2

Introducing Jesus, God, and the Holy Spirit . . . or Just God

YEARS AGO, I HAD a congregant in our church walk up with a small piece of paper with three words written on it: "God," "Jesus," "Holy Spirit." As he revealed his scrap of paper, he asked me this question: "Pastor Brandon, who do I pray to?" This young man, a mechanical engineer by trade, possessed a complex mind and was a deep thinker. I said, "Yes."

Before we individually unwrap who God, Jesus, and the Holy Spirit are, let's address a mystery of the Christian faith that has confounded theologians for centuries. That mystery, of course, is often phrased in a question similar to this: "How can three persons be one person at the same time?" Or, like my complex-minded engineer friend asked, "Who do I pray to?"

Often the word used in theological terms to describe God, Jesus, and the Holy Spirit is the Trinity. The course of study for this is often referred to as Trinitarian theology. For centuries Christ-followers have tried to find a language for our belief that God is God, that Jesus is God, and that the Holy Spirit is God. Yet we don't

Introducing Jesus, God, and the Holy Spirit... or Just God

worship three Gods—we worship only one God. Let me just say that the dialogue has not come without controversy!

One of my heroes of the faith is a guy named Athanasius. Strange name, big impact. He led a chorus of theologians and faith leaders in the fourth century attempting to establish a language for this mystery of the "threeness" of God and the "oneness" of God. Though likely not written by him, one early church creed bears his name and, more importantly, his theological understandings. Known as the Athanasian Creed, in it we find written of this mystery:

> That we worship one God in trinity and the trinity in unity, / neither blending their persons / nor dividing their essence. / For the person of the Father is a distinct person, / the person of the Son is another, / and that of the Holy Spirit still another. / But the divinity of the Father, Son, and Holy Spirit is one, / their glory equal, their majesty coeternal. . . . Thus the Father is God, / the Son is God, / the Holy Spirit is God. / Yet there are not three gods; / there is but one God.[1]

So, as we unpack the three persons of the Trinity below, please know that you are not alone if you find yourself unsure and a little confused about how to view and understand God, Jesus, and the Holy Spirit. You join millions of Christians around the world, and throughout history, who have, by faith, adopted this mystery the Bible outlines for us. Of course, God is God. But, is Jesus also God? Yes. Is the Holy Spirit God too? Yes. Who do we pray to then? I offer the same answer to you as I did to my brilliant engineer friend—yes!

---

1. Athanasius, "Athanasian Creed."

Who Is God?

"What comes to mind when we think about God is the most important thing about us."[2]

"Human thought falters and human language fails at defining God. But fortunately, God has revealed enough of himself to enable humans to understand some aspects of his being."[3]

I heard a cute joke some time ago about a little girl drawing a picture during art time in class. The conversation between her and her teacher went something like this:

> Teacher: "What are you drawing?"
> Little girl: "I'm drawing a picture of God."
> Teacher (chuckling): "How can you do that? No one knows what God looks like."
> Little girl: "They will when I'm done!"

No matter what I outline in the next few paragraphs about God, it won't be enough. You won't have a full picture. And, that is a good thing! For if God could be fully described in a few paragraphs I think we agree he would be an awfully tiny God, if God at all.

Among so many aspects of God that I could outline here, let me offer the following for your first few steps of faith. God is . . .

1. Transcendent and immanent
2. Good
3. Father
4. A pursuer of people

---

2. Tozer, *Knowledge of the Holy*, 1
3. Bilezikian, *Christianity 101*, 26.

Introducing Jesus, God, and the Holy Spirit . . . or Just God

Transcendent[4] and Immanent[5]

The Bible describes a God who is transcendent. One theologian describes God's transcendence this way: "This quality of God that represents him as prior to, distinct from, and not dependent on anything or anyone is called 'transcendence.'"[6] For instance, God is not bound by time; he lives outside of it. He is eternal; he transcends time.

Often the transcendence of God is described by theologians using "omni" terms. God is omniscient (all-knowing), God is omnipresent (everywhere present), and God is omnipotent (all-powerful). All true, and so much more.

However, the Bible also describes a God who is immanent. A God who is close, at hand, and pursuing his creation. All through Scripture, we witness the continued presence of God with his creation, his intervention, his direction, his healing, his persistent interest, and faithful love, most notably in Jesus' incarnation we talked about earlier. The God of the Bible is immanent.

Why is this important to us? God's immanence brings God close, doesn't it? The almighty, all-knowing God who transcends everyone, everything, everywhere for all time . . . is at once close. He searched for Adam and Eve in the garden of Eden (Gen 3:8), he called Abraham a friend and revealed his plans to him (Gen 18:17–19), he met with Moses (Exod 3), Solomon (1 Kgs 3), Mary (through the angel Gabriel in Luke 1), Joseph (Matt 1:20–25), the Samaritan woman (John 4), Paul (Acts 9), Peter (Acts 10), John (Rev 1), and so many others throughout Scripture.

God is close! And he is close to you in your joy, brokenheartedness, confusion, victories, defeats, goals, grieving, monumental moments, and every mistake.

---

4. "Of the Deity: In His being, exalted above and distinct from the universe; having transcendence." Oxford English Dictionary, "Transcendent."

5. "Existing or operating within; inherent; spec. (of God) permanently pervading and sustaining the universe." Oxford English Dictionary, "Immanent."

6. Bilezikian, *Christianity 101*, 26–27.

Good

I sense a forest of hands being raised in objection at this point. Hands representing some legitimate questions. Perhaps some that sound like this: "If God is good, why is there evil in the world?" While the purpose of this book is not to address the existence of evil, let me just say a few things. First, you join millions of others in asking this same question or some close variation of it. Second, while there is some compelling theological rationale that attempts to make sense of the existence of evil considering an all-powerful, completely good God (plenty of books and articles have attempted to tackle this issue), the exact reason why remains a mystery and will likely remain a mystery this side of heaven. Last, and I think most comforting and helpful, is that of all the religions of the world there is only one that boasts a God who enters the broken human condition to offer healing, answers, and comfort—Christianity. The cross of Jesus Christ is an enduring reminder of God's goodness, love, immanence (closeness), concern, relatability, and remedy to human suffering. We'll circle back to this idea of evil and suffering at the end of this section.

For now, on to God's goodness.

It is impossible to exaggerate how good God really is. And it's not just that God does good—he is good (Ps 119:68). Why is this important? Many reasons, not least of these is because what we believe matters. Why? Because our beliefs . . . what we truly choose to believe . . . informs our conduct. How we live, respond, pray, and treat others is all framed by our belief ecosystem.

If, for instance, we believe God is not good or only sort of good, then it's easy for us to blame him for the evil we see and experience. Further, it impacts our worship. Why would we worship a God we believe is not completely good and who is capable of evil? I heard a pastor one time say, "If I treated my kids the way some people believe God treats his kids, I'd be arrested for child abuse."

Introducing Jesus, God, and the Holy Spirit... or Just God

Defining "Good"

Language matters. If language matters, then the definition of words within language must matter. I can hear a question scratching at the back of your mind: "Brandon, what do you mean by 'good?'" My definition doesn't matter nearly as much as the biblical definition. One note here: between the Hebrew Old Testament and the Greek New Testament, the Bible uses multiple words for "good," where our English language uses one.

If we begin with the Old Testament, we find the word "Tov"[7] is used over seven hundred times. It's a pregnant word describing something or someone as "very good," "perfect," "harmony," "masterpiece," "rich," "valuable in estimation," "becoming," "happy," and "prosperous," and many more English words could be used to describe the full breadth of this one word.

Of God, the psalmist wrote, "You are good and do good; Teach me Your statutes."[8]

Of the way God pursues us, the psalmist wrote, "Yes, goodness and faithful love will pursue me all the days of my life, and I will live in the LORD's house as long as I live."[9]

God noted about his creation (including you!), "God saw everything he had made: it was supremely good."[10]

In the Greek New Testament, the prevailing word used for our English word "good" is "agathos," a versatile word used over one hundred times in the New Testament meaning "excellence of many kinds"; it's used to describe "fertile soil" (Luke 8), "productive trees" (Matt 7), the produce or fruit of the Spirit of God (Gal 5:22) that he produces in us, as well as the type of work God has designed us to accomplish (Eph 2:10). Listen to how this is worded in Ephesians:

---

7. Tov: pronounced "t-oh-ve."
8. Ps 119:68 (CEB).
9. Ps 23:6 (CEB).
10. Gen 1:31 (CEB).

> Instead, we are God's accomplishment, created in Christ Jesus to do good things. God planned for these good things to be the way that we live our lives.[11]

Instead of the word "accomplishment," one translation says we are God's "masterpiece!" And God has designed us to do good—excellent things—as a way of life.

Finally, Jesus is the ultimate example of goodness in Scripture. Just spend some time reading the Gospels (Matthew, Mark, Luke, and John), and you'll find Jesus healing the sick, delivering people of evil spirits, raising the dead, calming storms, befriending sinners, and defending the vulnerable. Further, he forgives, restores, teaches, encourages, admonishes, expresses compassion, and takes the time to listen to people. All he does is "tov." All he does is "agathos." Not once in Scripture do we see Jesus giving someone a disease, or causing a storm, or demonizing someone.

Jesus was, is, did, and does good!

Why then do things that are not good happen to us? Why the suffering, trauma, death? Good question. Let's address this briefly.

Addressing the Real Problem

My pastor used to say all the time, "Unmet expectations create frustration and anger every time." You see, what happens when we follow God with our whole heart and then our spouse files for divorce? Or we see on the news Christians around the world being persecuted and killed? Or we're forced to live with the abuse from our childhood? Or a parent stands over the coffin of their child, rather than the other way around?

If we're honest, deep down we have this expectation that God would keep us from all this evil and suffering. What would fuel this expectation? Well, we believe that God is good, and not only that, but he is all-powerful. So, it seems reasonable for us to expect God to come through for good on our behalf. In other words, God

---

11. Eph 2:10 (CEB).

Introducing Jesus, God, and the Holy Spirit... or Just God

has not met our definition of good. And so, we often become frustrated and angry with God.

Our definition of good seems to be that God protects me from all that is not good, from anything that might involve suffering and loss and pain.

Let me address three things related to this that may help you on your faith journey: (a) Jesus never promised a pain-free life in his invitation to follow him, (b) we must acknowledge the mystery of letter "a" above, and (c) no one understands our suffering more than Jesus.

Let's take them briefly one at a time:

a. Jesus never promised a pain-free life in his invitation to follow him.

In fact, he promised just the opposite:

> Jesus said to everyone, "All who want to come after me must say no to themselves, take up their cross daily, and follow me."[12]

> I've said these things to you so that you will have peace in me. In the world you have distress. But be encouraged! I have conquered the world.[13]

> If you belonged to the world, the world would love you as its own. However, I have chosen you out of the world, and you don't belong to the world. This is why the world hates you. Remember what I told you, "Servants aren't greater than their master." If the world harassed me, it will harass you too. If it kept my word, it will also keep yours. The world will do all these things to you on account of my name, because it doesn't know the one who sent me.[14]

Of the twelve apostles Jesus invited to follow him, and who decided to do so, Scripture and history reveals ten of them were

---

12. Luke 9:23 (CEB).
13. John 16:33 (CEB).
14. John 15:19–21 (CEB).

murdered for their faith, one was imprisoned in a hard-labor camp as an old man for his faith until his death, and one committed suicide.

Further, if you read the story of the apostle Paul (take a look at 2 Cor 11), who wrote at least two-thirds of the New Testament, you'll find he was beaten with rods multiple times, whipped, chased from town to town by people who wanted him dead, imprisoned multiple times, beaten and left for dead, faced starvation, was pelted with stones at least three times, abandoned cold and naked, shipwrecked multiple times, and more.

No, we were never promised a safe, risk-free, painless life. We were promised just the opposite. This doesn't mean that God is not good.

b.   We must acknowledge the mystery of letter "a" above.

Perhaps a look at an example from the Bible may help. In the Old Testament, there is this man named Job who loved God (not just by his own admission, but by God's admission), and in one day is systematically dismantled by the enemy. He loses his wealth (livestock and servants), as well as each of his adult children. Further, he lost his personal health and was afflicted with painful boils all over his body. And if that wasn't enough, instead of grieving with him and comforting him, his wife meets him with this statement, "Are you still clinging to your integrity? Curse God, and die."[15]

Uh, marriage counseling anyone? As you read on in Job's journey, you find that what he really wants is an audience with God to question him about all the suffering that has been brought on him. Isn't this the human response for many of us in our suffering? We have a few questions! "Why is this happening?" "What have I done so wrong to deserve this?" "Why do bad things happen to good people, and good things happen to bad people?" "Why has God forsaken me?" (Jesus himself asked this question.) We'd like an audience with the all-powerful God who could have prevented this, and who could at least stop it. And, at the very least, provide answers for all the pain.

---

15. Job 2:9 (CEB).

Introducing Jesus, God, and the Holy Spirit... or Just God

Well, Job indeed receives what he wants. God shows up to Job. Finally! At least now we'll get some answers to this horror show. What's interesting is that God does speak and clears up some things, except for one thing—the answer as to why all this happened to Job. Job is still left with the mystery of why he had to suffer so severely.

Friend, it's important you hear this early in your journey with Jesus—there will likely be pain in your life you will not have an answer for this side of heaven. There will remain a mystery to some pain and suffering. Perhaps you can take some comfort in letter "c" below.

c.   No one understands our suffering more than Jesus.

Christianity is the only world religion that boasts a God who humbled himself, became one of his creations, and suffered with and for them (more on this in the next chapter). Jesus wept (Luke 19:41; John 11:35; Heb 5:7), stood at the tomb of one of his best friends (John 11), was rejected and betrayed (Luke 22:47–48; Matt 26:56; John 6:66), rejected by his family (John 7:5), harassed by the religious elite, and finally in a bloody, gory scene suffered the most excruciating execution ever devised in the human mind. As Christ-followers, we can never say, "God does not understand my suffering." Jesus understands our plight intimately, not just because he is all-knowing, but because he chose to walk the journey of sorrow, pain, rejection, and death himself.

In all this, God is totally, completely, beautifully good, perhaps most because of his own suffering.

Father

Here again, I sense strong resistance from some who have few pleasant memories (if any) of their earthly father. Understood. Unfortunately, there are far too many in this camp.

We've already established God is good; therefore, if he is a father, he must be a good one. In the most famous sermon ever preached, Jesus was talking about prayer and he revealed this about his goodness and desire to share it with his creation: "If you who are evil know how to give good gifts to your children, how much more will your heavenly Father give good things to those who ask him."[16]

Where do we get this idea of God being a "father?" From the Bible! In the Old Testament, the word "father" is used over 600 times, and less than ten times does God allow it to be used to describe himself as a father—about 1.6 percent of the time. In the New Testament, the word "father" is used about 311 times and of those God allows it to be used by the writers roughly 249 times to describe himself as a dad—about 80 percent of the time! As we move from the Old Testament to the New, clearly God is sending a message about what kind of relationship he desires to have with us.

In fact, both Paul and Jesus used an endearing term when relating to and talking with God. The word is "abba" (Mark 14:36; Rom 8:15; Gal 4:6). In twenty-first-century Jewish culture, the word would have an English translation similar to "papa," or "daddy." While the exact meaning may have been slightly different two thousand years ago, it was nonetheless a deeply familial, close, and intimate term.

As a good earthly father is patient, kind, strong, protective, a provider, an instructor, so too is our heavenly Father . . . and so much more.

A Pursuer of People

Just a few thoughts on this. A critical theme you'll find as you begin to read the Bible is that God is constantly pursuing his creation. He pursued Adam and Eve in the garden of Eden. He pursued Abraham, Isaac, Jacob, and then his people through a deliverer named Moses. He then pursued and led his people for forty years in the desert. He pursued them through leaders the Bible refers to as "judges" (give the book of Judges a read sometime), who would

---

16. Matt 7:11 (CEB).

Introducing Jesus, God, and the Holy Spirit . . . or Just God

rise and help deliver God's people from oppression caused by their own disobedience!

Further, God continued to pursue his people through the leadership of the kings of the Old Testament, and even through the prophets of the Old Testament.

If all this wasn't enough, in the most mind-blowing act in human history, God chose to pursue his creation by becoming a human being in the person of Jesus Christ! Even more, God continues to pursue his creation through the person of the Holy Spirit (John 14–16).

Finally, God will consummate his pursuit of his creation by returning a second time to gather up those who have placed their faith in him (John 14:3).

This is not just something he does—it is who he is—Immanuel, God with us, guiding us, teaching us, loving us, helping us. He is a pursuer of people, and he has been, and will continue to pursue you!

Who Was Jesus—the Man?

> "With Jesus, it's easy to be complicated and hard to be simple. Part of the difficulty is that Jesus was and is much, much more than people imagine."[17]

The million-dollar question! We do know his last name was not "Christ." This was a Jewish term to describe a coming messiah, a savior. For others "Christ" is a swear word (I know, not for you). I had a friend who worked construction and for months he would show up to work to the pejorative mockery of his friend asking, "So, how's your *Jesus Christ* today?" Who was the historical Jesus who breathed first-century air, walked the dusty roads of Palestine, felt pain, was angered, laughed, cried, and experienced death?

In his book *Who Is This Man?: The Unmistakable Impact of the Inescapable Jesus*, John Ortberg reminds his readers that for most people in history, their impact on society fades in direct

17. Wright, *Simply Jesus*, 4

correlation to the amount of time they've been dead.[18] So, our impact on society will be less one hundred years after our death than just five years after our death, for example. Not so with Jesus. This man, who Christ-followers and non-Christ-followers alike agree lived in the first century AD, has an ascending popularity curve. Jesus has more followers in more places than at any point in the last two thousand years. How can this be? Who is this man?

There's so much we could say here but let me throw a highlighter on just a few things. According to biblical tradition, Jesus was a Jew born in a barn to an unwed teenage mom, under Roman occupation.

Scripture indicates that he had siblings, and his father was a carpenter who likely taught him the same trade. According to Scripture, we know more about his birth, teaching/healing ministry and events surrounding his death, than we do about his childhood, teenage or early-adult years.

He began his rabbinical ministry around the age of 30 and invited (as was customary for rabbis) several students (disciples) to join him in his ministry. A quick scan of who Jesus invited to follow him seems to indicate he wasn't terribly picky about his company (good news for me and you). Among the crew were a few loud-mouthed fishermen, some nationalistic zealots, a scumbag tax collector (at the very opposite end of the political spectrum from the zealots on the same team by the way), an ambivalent doubter, and a thief and traitor among others. You'll find as you read about Jesus' life in Matthew, Mark, Luke, and John, his time with these jokers was every bit as tumultuous as their stations and professions indicate. In fact, they all fled in fear when it seemed he needed them the most.

According to Scripture, he was arrested under false pretense, placed on Roman trial for the accusation of blasphemy[19] and in-

---

18. Ortberg, *Who Is This Man*, 11

19. Blasphemy for the Jew, in essence, is any act or speech that contradicts their religion. At his trial, they accused Jesus of claiming to be God. In fact, several times during his ministry, Jews attempted to kill him for it.

Introducing Jesus, God, and the Holy Spirit ... or Just God

surrection.[20] The Roman governor, Pontius Pilate, eventually abdicated his duty to render a decision to the whims of an angry mob who called for Jesus to be crucified. And he was.

Since it was a Roman trial, it garnered a Roman method of death—crucifixion. Based on the scars on his hands and feet, Jesus was nailed to two pieces of wood in the shape of a cross to accommodate his hands stretched out and his feet hanging down. After he died, his body was embalmed and buried in a borrowed tomb.

According to Scripture, he was only in the borrowed tomb for three days. Miraculously, he rose from the dead and appeared to hundreds of people for over a month before he ascended to heaven.

This idea of Jesus rising from the dead kicks wide open the door for us to talk about who Jesus is today. Right? If indeed he somehow, against all human logic, overcame death, then we at least need to step up to the edge of that idea and peer in.

As mentioned earlier, it is important to remember that it's not only the Bible that offers an account of Jesus in history, additional historians of the first and second century like Josephus and Tacitus (among others) affirm the scriptural account of Jesus' life, teaching, healings, and even his resurrection from the dead according to Christian tradition.

Who Is Jesus—the One True God?

Let me reason with you for just a moment. If Jesus didn't rise from the dead, wouldn't that make him just another footnote in history? Albeit an influential one, but a footnote nonetheless. A cool guy, amazing teacher, an example to live by maybe ... but just another human being who lived and died. I think we agree. There is only one small (by small I mean massive) problem with this idea—he claimed to be God! He claimed to have the ability to forgive sins (Mark 2: 5–7; only God can do that), he claimed that he lived long before Moses (John 8:58; only an eternal being could live

---

20. Insurrection for the Roman citizen, in essence, would be any act or speech in direct opposition or competition to Caesar or the empire. Jesus' claim to divinity would be viewed as a direct threat to Caesar's rule.

thousands of years), he claimed to be equal with God (John 5:17–18), he claimed "oneness" with God (John 10:30; which the religious elite immediately tried to kill him for since he was claiming equality with God), and he told God-seekers to look no further than himself to see the true God (John 14:9; how arrogant is that!).

Imagine if one of your coworkers walked up to you and said, "Listen, if you're on a search for God, you need not look any further than *mwah*!" You may have all kinds of labels for them, but a "good teacher," a "solid moral example," or "a prophet" would not make the list. The list of labels we afford someone claiming to be God is a short, non-flattering list indeed.

Let's continue reasoning. If Jesus did claim to be God according to Scripture, then aren't we left with only a few conclusions? First conclusion: he's crazy. This is likely the first label we attribute to someone claiming to be God, isn't it? Your messiah-complex coworker above would be summarily dismissed, if not transported to a local psychiatric ward for mental health analysis and care. One important note: Jesus' family did not believe his claim to be God during his earthly ministry. Yet, as mentioned earlier, eventually his half-brother, James, wrote a book of the Bible describing Jesus as his "Lord." What changed? The resurrection. Right? If someone claims to be God, predicts their own death, their resurrection, and then pulls it off . . . doesn't this change the game? Second conclusion: he was lying. And, through this lie, he was able to pull off the greatest hoax in the history of humanity since he now has more followers in more places than at any point in history. Think about the implications of this conclusion. Billions and billions of people over the last two thousand years have been gullible enough to fall for the greatest hoax to ever be perpetrated on humanity . . . including the author of this book. Third conclusion: he *is* God. If Jesus was God two thousand years ago, then he is God today. And if he is God today, this changes everything. It means he is alive, that all his teachings are true, that there is a new, better way to live. It means there is nothing he can't do, his promises are true, and that he is the Savior of humanity . . . among thousands of other things we could say about who Jesus is today. But, since you've picked this

Introducing Jesus, God, and the Holy Spirit... or Just God

book up, I bet you've likely had some sort of experience or sober reasoning session (or both) that has made our third conclusion the only viable, likely conclusion to make.

Who Is the Holy Spirit?

> "The Holy Spirit has long been the Cinderella of the Trinity. The other two sisters may have gone to the theological ball; the Holy Spirit got left behind every time."[21]

What comes to your mind when you read the words "Holy Spirit?" Or, better yet... "Holy Ghost?" Is it some charismatic TV preacher? Or perhaps people falling down when the same TV preacher touches (shoves) them? Or perhaps just the word "ghost" elicits all kinds of weird imagery for you. Let's be honest, who wants to have any kind of close relationship with a ghost! Whatever your view, or lack thereof, of the Holy Spirit, I have found he has either received little attention (the Cinderella of the ball), or a bad rap altogether due to poor teaching and representation by well-meaning Christ-followers.

So, who is the Holy Spirit, and what does the Holy Spirit do? Among many things I could share with you, let me address four things that will help you along your first steps of faith.

The Holy Spirit Is God

We addressed this earlier in the chapter and I don't need to repeat all that has been said. However, let me attempt to punctuate this truth with some of the final words of Jesus.

Goodbyes are hard for me. I remember clearly the morning of November 21, 2005. My wife, Joy, and I, along with our two little kids—eight years and five years—were headed to California to take on a new ministry assignment. We were leaving our hometown, our family, all our friends, and frankly all we knew to head to a

---

21. McGrath, *Christian Theology*, 434.

place we almost knew nothing about, and where we knew no one. I stood in the driveway, moving truck brimming with our earthly possessions, surrounded by family, and I began to cry. Then the crying became a cascade of the wrinkled-face, snot-running, ugly-face, booger bawling. I wonder if you've been in this place.

We had just purchased a beautiful new home about eight months earlier, our kids had best friends, most of our family was in our hometown, and frankly we loved where we lived! I questioned my decision-making, what the move would do to my kids, the impact on my wife, whether I had the skill set for this new post, and so much more. It was a rough goodbye.

In the closing chapters of the Gospel of John, we find Jesus sharing an evening meal with his disciples. In Jewish culture it's known as the Passover meal and is one of their main annual celebrations. I encourage you to ask the pastor of the church you attend about it. There are many things going on in these final chapters of the book of John, not least of which is Jesus explaining to his friends that he is leaving. This is goodbye for now. In fact, Jesus makes this statement as part of his farewell: "I assure you that it is better for you that I go away."[22] What an odd statement. Put yourself in the footsteps of the disciples. Jesus has been with them for about three and a half years, and in this time he taught them, laughed with them, cried with them, challenged them, performed miracles in front of them and through them, comforted them, encouraged them, rescued them, and was available when they had questions about any of it. They had to be thinking, "Explain to us how in the world it could be better for us if you leave!"

In another part of his farewell address, he says this:

> I will ask the Father, and he will send another Companion, who will be with you forever.[23]

First, notice the word "Companion." In some translations the word is "Advocate," in another translation the word is "Helper," and in still another the word is "Counselor." All of these English

---

22. John 16:7 (CEB).
23. John 14:16 (CEB).

words are helpful descriptors of the original Greek word used. Essentially the word means "one called alongside to help." This is the function of the Holy Spirit.

Second, notice the word just before it: "another." If we're not careful, we can run right past it. The word means "one beside, another of the same kind." We also see in the meaning based on how Jesus uses it, "one beside Me and in addition to Me, but one just like me." Based on this, Jesus is essentially saying this: "He will do in my absence what I would do if I were physically present with you."

Why would Jesus say this? Because not only is he (Jesus) God, but the Holy Spirit is God too. And, just like Jesus was a companion, teacher, and comforter to the disciples, so too would the Holy Spirit be.

The Holy Spirit Is For Everyone

There is a key distinction between the Old Testament portion of the Bible and the New Testament portion of the Bible.

Briefly, we certainly see the work of the Holy Spirit in the Old Testament, but only in and through certain people, at certain times, for certain things. For example, we see the Spirit coming upon a guy named Bezalel in Exod 31. The Bible says that he was full of the Spirit of God and uniquely gifted as a craftsman for the work of the temple.

But in the New Testament, we see the Holy Spirit is no longer for certain people, at certain times, for certain things. Rather, we are told that the Spirit is for everyone, at all times. In Acts 2, the apostle Peter stands up on the day of Pentecost (another key Jewish annual celebration) to explain what the crowds were seeing, hearing, and experiencing when God chose to send the beautiful gift of his Spirit upon his people. The crowd had questions, and ultimately asked what they needed to do to receive the Holy Spirit:

> When the crowd heard this, they were deeply troubled. They said to Peter and the other apostles, "Brothers, what should we do?" Peter replied, "Change your hearts and lives. Each of you must be baptized in the name of Jesus Christ for the forgiveness of your sins. Then you will receive the gift of the Holy Spirit. This promise is for you, your children, and for all who are far away—as many as the Lord our God invites."[24]

Notice the words "far away." Another translation uses the words "far off." This word includes both geographic distance and time distance. Those who geographically could not make it to the celebration feast on the day of Pentecost, and those chronologically in time who could not make it to the party (you and me!).

The Holy Spirit is no longer for certain people, at certain times, for certain things (Old Testament), rather he is for all who call on the name of Jesus, at all times!

The Holy Spirit Is a Person!

"How can a spirit be a person?" you might ask. Fair question. Let's start right there with the name given to this person of the triune (three yet one) God. What's in a name anyway?

Your Bible is written largely in two languages: the Old Testament in Hebrew and the New Testament in Greek. Over eight hundred times we see the name "Holy Spirit" or "Holy Ghost" used. And why this happened is because when it came to translating the name of the Holy Spirit into English, our translators were left with a dilemma. There really is no English word that adequately captures the original language used for Spirit in the Bible.

The Old Testament Hebrew word used is "Ruwach," which translates roughly to "a wind," "a breath," "a violent exhalation," or "a blast of breath." Notice, it's neither "Spirit" nor "Ghost!"

Here is an example from Genesis: "In the beginning, God created the heavens and the earth. The earth was without form and void, and darkness was over the face of the deep. And the Spirit

---

24. Acts 2:37–39 (CEB).

Introducing Jesus, God, and the Holy Spirit . . . or Just God

[wind, breath, violent exhalation, blast of breath] of God was hovering over the face of the waters."[25]

Let's look at the New Testament. The Greek New Testament word is "Pneuma," which translates roughly to "current of air," "blast of breath," "a strong breeze."

Pneumatic tools, anyone? Again, we can't have God the Father, God the Son, and God "the strong breeze." Just doesn't quite fit. So "Spirit" was the English word chosen.

But just because God is Spirit doesn't mean he is not a person. Jesus says in John 16:13, "However, when He, the Spirit of truth, has come, He will guide you into all truth; for He will not speak on His own authority, but whatever He hears He will speak; and He will tell you things to come" (NKJV). Notice Jesus doesn't say "when the ghost comes" or "when 'it' comes." He uses a personal pronoun when talking about the Holy Spirit. The Spirit is a person, not some disembodied ghost that does ghostly things, but a Spirit who performs human functions.

Speaking of human function, we find in Scripture the Holy Spirit does indeed perform functions that a person performs. Here are just a few:

- He loves (Rom 15:30).
- He has intellect (1 Cor 2:10–11).
- He has a will (1 Cor 12:11).
- He has emotions: he can be grieved, insulted, and he can rejoice (Luke 10:21; 1 Thess 1:6–7; Heb 10:29; Eph 4:30).
- He teaches (John 14:26).
- He tells the truth (John 16:13–15).
- He comforts (John 14:16–18).
- He convicts (John 16:8).
- He guides (John 14:16; 16:13).
- He prays (Rom 8:26–27).

25. Gen 1:1–2 (ESV).

The Holy Spirit is a person, and longs to have a relationship with you.

The Purpose of Being Filled with the Spirit: Spirit-Empowered Witness (Acts 1:8)

In Acts 19, we find this interesting account of Paul's travels:

> While Apollos was in Corinth, Paul took a route through the interior and came to Ephesus, where he found some disciples. He asked them, "Did you receive the Holy Spirit when you came to believe?"[26]

These disciples answer Paul by telling him they had not even heard that there was such a thing as a Holy Spirit. He then baptized them, and prayed for them that they might receive the Holy Spirit.

So, let's address this question: "Why would I need to receive the Holy Spirit?" Depending on what church you are connected with, they may ask the question this way: "Why would someone need to be baptized in the Spirit?," or "Why would someone need to be filled with the Spirit?"

There are many reasons. Probably at the top of the list is this: for Spirit-empowered witness to the world.

Again, in the book of Acts, the author quotes the words of Jesus before he ascended to heaven after his resurrection:

> Rather, you will receive power when the Holy Spirit has come upon you, and you will be my witnesses in Jerusalem, in all Judea and Samaria, and to the end of the earth.[27]

In a moment I want to lead you in a prayer to receive the Holy Spirit. Before I do, I want to punctuate this all-important point: the purpose of receiving—being filled, being baptized in—the Spirit is so we can be supernaturally empowered by God to share and minister the good news of Jesus Christ.

---

26. Acts 19:1–2 (CEB).
27. Acts 1:8 (CEB).

Introducing Jesus, God, and the Holy Spirit ... or Just God

One last thing before we pray. There is often confusion about when a Christ-follower receives the Holy Spirit. First, I encourage you to have a conversation with your pastor as questions arise. Second, let me give you two truths from Scripture that will help answer this question. The apostle Paul wrote a letter to believers living in a place called Ephesus (modern-day Turkey) and he encouraged them this way:

> You too heard the word of truth in Christ, which is the good news of your salvation. You were sealed with the promised Holy Spirit because you believed in Christ. The Holy Spirit is the down payment on our inheritance, which is applied toward our redemption as God's own people, resulting in the honor of God's glory.[28]

So, we see here that a person receives the Holy Spirit when they hear the gospel and choose to believe in and follow Jesus. Praise God! That's the first truth; let me share with you the second one. In the same letter Paul said this a few chapters later:

> Don't get drunk on wine, which produces depravity. Instead, be filled with the Spirit in the following ways.[29]

If we were to take a close look at the original language in this verse, it could easily be interpreted something close to this: "Be in a continual state of being filled with the Holy Spirit." In fact, notice how the Amplified translation of the Bible interprets this verse for us:

> Do not get drunk with wine, for that is wickedness (corruption, stupidity), but be filled with the [Holy] Spirit and constantly guided by Him.[30]

What I want you to see is that if you have chosen to believe in Jesus, you received the Holy Spirit, and that you need his empowerment, help, and comfort every day. In other words, there is an ongoing, daily filling of the Spirit available to you as well. Again, praise God!

28. Eph 1:13–14 (CEB); see also John 7:39.
29. Eph 5:18 (CEB).
30. Eph 5:18 (AMP).

The Most Ancient Prayer of the Church

Most theologians would argue that the New Testament church was born on the day of Pentecost (Acts 2). The context into which God poured out his Spirit on Pentecost was one of unity and prayer among the early Christ-followers (Acts 1:14—2:1).

In one form or another, for thousands of years, the most ancient prayer of the church is simply this: "Come, Holy Spirit."

If you have decided to follow Jesus, perhaps I could lead you in a similar prayer? Take a moment on your own, or with the person you are reading this book with, and pray this prayer from your heart. When you have finished, take some time to create some space for the Spirit to respond to you. Let's pray:

> Jesus, I believe in you. Thank you for sealing me with your precious Spirit. You said in Luke 11 that our heavenly Father is a good parent and loves to give gifts to his kids, including the gift of the Holy Spirit to those who ask. And Ephesians encourages me to be filled everyday with your Spirit. So, I'm asking. Please fill me with your precious Spirit today. I need your comfort, counsel, help, and empowerment. Come, Holy Spirit.

CHAPTER 2 DISCUSSION QUESTIONS:

1. What attribute of God described in this chapter encourages you the most? Are there any that are disruptive? Why?
2. Is it helpful to know there are sources outside of the Bible that give testimony to the life, death, and resurrection of Jesus?
3. Why do you think Jesus is more popular and has more followers today than at any point in history?
4. When you think about how the main purpose of being filled with the Spirit is so that we can be empowered to share the gospel (the good news of Jesus) with others, what comes to mind?

3

Introducing the Bible

"The entire Bible, even the stories of the Old Testament, are pointing us to Jesus Christ, to who he is and what he has done for humanity."[1]

BEFORE I ANSWER SOME key questions in this chapter about the Bible, let me acknowledge several preceding questions that need to be addressed first. Most of them revolve around one key question: can the Bible be trusted?

There are various reasons people ask this question. Some have to do with what they feel are outdated cultural aspects of the Bible and, for others, they feel they've identified contradictions in the Bible—just to name a couple.

I admit that I'm jumping over this question with the assumption that if you've shifted your weight this far, you believe not only Jesus can be trusted, but the Bible as well. However, I want to recommend a few books to you, among many, that address this very question: can the Bible be trusted? First, chapter 3 of Mark Clark's book, *The Problem of God*, is a wonderful apologetic for the trustworthiness of Scripture. Second, Amy Orr-Ewing's book, *Why Trust the Bible?*, is an excellent resource. Last, chapter 7 of

---

1. Clark, *Problem of God*, 83.

Timothy Keller's book, *The Reason for God*, is a solid resource in answering some of the most challenging questions thrown at the Bible.

What Is the Bible?

What is this book—these ancient writings that have been banned, burned, and beloved for hundreds, even thousands, of years? What is this book we hold in our hands today that consists of sixty-six different books, written by around forty authors, written over the course of about 1,500 years, and is the number-one best-selling book of all time (without a close runner-up)?

At its core, the Bible is the story of God. More specifically, it is the story of God's movement in, and love and redemptive purposes for, humanity. From Genesis to Revelation, we see God's pursuit of his creation. Further, the central figure in God's redemptive story is Jesus.

The collective story the Bible tells is one that does not shy away from pain, heartbreak, confusion, questioning God, family drama, and the depths to which the depravity of human beings plunge to serve their own self-interests. Because of this, the Bible often becomes a mirror reflecting the depths of our own souls as well.

What Version of the Bible Should I Read?

As you become more familiar with the Bible, you will likely find some strong opinions regarding which version of the Bible one should read and which they shouldn't read. Let me attempt to add some clarity to what you might hear.

First, I think it is noteworthy to mention that almost all commonly read versions of the Bible have been developed by a team of highly competent specialists. Professionals in research, editing, theology, Jewish history, church history, biblical languages, and more. These folks are not only highly skilled in their area of expertise, but deeply committed to the integrity of the biblical text.

Second, the task of translating one language to another is challenging, and in some cases can be extremely challenging. I have a friend from Calabar, a city in Nigeria, Africa, who is an author. She was visiting our home and talking about her latest book. She was writing it in English largely for a US audience, but it was about some of the deep spiritual needs in her hometown of Calabar. At one point in the conversation, as she was attempting to describe a word in her native culture of Africa, she stopped and couldn't go on. She must have stared at the floor for three or four minutes in silence trying to find words in English to describe the meaning of this African word. And guess what, she could not find the words.

Now, layer in the task of translation, not just from the same period of time as my friend was attempting to do, but from an ancient culture to a modern one. You can see how this can become extremely complex very quickly. With this in mind, let's look at just one aspect of the process of Bible translation that creates sticking points for our translators. We'll call it the idiomatic problem, or the problem with idioms.

Let's begin with a working definition:

> Idiom: A form of expression, grammatical construction, phrase, etc., used in a distinctive way in a particular language, dialect, or language variety; spec. a group of words established by usage as having a meaning not deducible from the meanings of the individual words.[2]

Here are a few cultural idioms generally understood in the United States, with their translation in parenthesis:

"Let's call it a day." (Let's stop working.)

"I'm in over my head." (I don't know what I'm doing.)

It's important to remember, as the definition above highlights, every culture has its own idiomatic language often without a direct English translation or understanding, and the Hebrew/

---

2. Oxford English Dictionary, "Idiom."

Weight Shift

Jewish/Roman culture of the Bible is no different. Let me give you a couple of examples.

Often when the New Testament speaks of people who were sick, the literal reading of the Greek text is "having it badly." Therefore, a literal reading of Matt 4:24 would be, "And they brought to him all the ones having it badly with various diseases and torments."[3] Since this would not make sense to an English reader, one translation of the Bible renders this idiomatic language this way: "News about him spread throughout Syria. People brought to him all those who had various kinds of diseases, those in pain, those possessed by demons, those with epilepsy, and those who were paralyzed, and he healed them."[4]

Another famous idiom is found in 1 Pet 1:13 where it literally says, "Gird [or girding] up the loins of your mind." This literal translation is meaningless because it contains an idiomatic expression that makes no literal sense—our mind does not have loins! The expression means "pay attention," or "prepare for action."[5]

So you can imagine the dilemma our Bible translators often find themselves in as they do the hard work of translating the Bible into various languages. Further, in addition to cultural idioms, there are simply some Hebrew and Greek words that do not have an English equivalent—we just covered a big one, "Holy Spirit!"

With these two considerations (and several more) in mind, we find pastors, theologians, and biblical scholars will often categorize Bible translations into three general "buckets": formal translations, functional translations, and free translations. Let's take them briefly one at a time.

One quick note here: most modern English translations fall somewhere on a spectrum between formal and functional, or between functional and free, avoiding a strict adherence to any one philosophy of translation.

---

3. Stewart, "What Are the Major Theories," para. 7.
4. CEB.
5. Stewart, "What Are the Major Theories," para. 10.

Formal

The formal translations generally maintain an adherence to the literal translation of the original text. The benefit here is obvious: the English translation of the original language (Hebrew, Aramaic, or Greek) is as close to the original meaning as our translators could get. However, what happens when there is not an equivalent English word translation for the original language? The downside of some formal translations is they can often be clunky and confusing to read. Our English translators do their best to translate meaning from one language to another, even when there isn't an exact English translation. Further, because of the idiom (not idiot) problem outlined above, there technically is no such thing as a pure, word-for-word, formal translation of the Bible, for even our formal translators must reword the idiomatic language of other cultures for the English reader.

Some translations of the Bible that often make the formal translation list are the King James Version, American Standard Version, Young's Literal Translation, the New American Bible, the New King James Version, and some lists even include the English Standard Version.

Functional

Most of our functional translators are concerned less with a formal word-for-word translation and more with a phrase-for-phrase interpretation of the Bible. Why? To help ensure the Scriptures are understandable. Readability and understandability are two gifts most functional translations give us.

Let's look at an example that compares Ps 23:5(b) in two different versions, one formal and one functional:

> Formal: New King James Version (NKJV)
>
> You anoint my head with oil; / My cup runs over.

Functional: New Living Translation (NLT)

> You honor me by anointing my head with oil. / My cup overflows with blessings.

Notice, if someone unfamiliar with the Bible were reading the New King James Version, they may be left with some questions about what "anointing" someone's "head with oil" means. What does this signify? The translators of the New Living Translation attempt to remove the barrier of confusion by letting the reader know that this was a cultural way to honor a guest. Instead of looking at each individual word, they looked at the entire phrase and asked, "What is this phrase, steeped in cultural significance, attempting to communicate?"

What are the disadvantages? What if the translators misunderstand a cultural idiom or practice? What if they misunderstand the cultural practice of anointing someone's head with oil? Clearly then, the English translation runs the risk of missing the mark and adding additional confusion.

A few examples of translations that usually wind up on this functional list are the Common English Bible, the New International Version, the New Living Translation, and the Holman Christian Standard Bible, among others.

Free

By "free" this does not mean "free to interpret however one wants"; rather, free to maintain fidelity to Scripture while using a thought-for-thought method of translation (versus word-for-word, or phrase-for-phrase). And, we needed to complete our alliteration of Christian-approved F-words—formal, functional, free! What is the main benefit of this translation? Readability for sure. Let's look at the same verse using a free translation:

Formal: New King James Version (NKJV)

> You anoint my head with oil; / My cup runs over.

Introducing the Bible

Functional: New Living Translation (NLT)

> You honor me by anointing my head with oil. / My cup overflows with blessings.

Free: Good News Translation (GNT)

> You welcome me as an honored guest / and fill my cup to the brim.

Notice, the Good News Translation analyzes the "thought" of anointing one's head with oil and translates this cultural practice by providing an equivalent modern-day "thought."

But again, what are the disadvantages? Very similar to those of the functional translations of the Bible. What if the translators misunderstand the core cultural aspects of what the biblical writers were attempting to communicate?

A few examples of translations that usually wind up on this free list are The Message, the Good News Translation, the New Century Version, and The Passion Translation, among others.

You might be saying at this point, "Brandon, you still haven't answered your own question: which version of the Bible should I read?" You're right. I wanted to give a brief overview of Bible translations because I have received this question a lot as a pastor.

The answer is—to use one of our cultural idioms—not so cut and dried. And, I'm not sure there is a one-size-fits-all (no way, another idiom!) answer either. I would encourage you to consider the answer to a few questions: How familiar are you with the Bible? What is your learning style? How is your reading and comprehension? Is there a version your pastor reads from or recommends? Your answers here may help inform whether you begin with a more free translation, or jump right in with a more formal translation.

I know folks who change reading translations each year, others who rotate through a list of translations each week as they study the Bible, and still others who stick with their favorite translation and simply use the others for reference on occasion, if they are attempting to get a better sense of a particular passage.

There are several free Bible apps that allow you to switch between multiple versions as you read and compare verses. This is a great way to explore which translation might be best for you. Most important . . . ask the Holy Spirit to guide you.

How Should I Read It?

I just typed in the search bar of Amazon, "How to read the Bible." Here is a quick list of only a few results:

- *How to Read the Bible for All Its Worth* (I've read this one, and it's pretty good!)
- *How to Read the Bible: As If Your Life Depends on It*
- *How to Read the Bible Well: What It Is, What It Isn't, and How to Love It (Again)*
- *How (Not) to Read the Bible*
- *How to Study the Bible*
- *How to Read the Bible Like a Seminary Professor*
- *How to Read the Bible Through the Jesus Lens*

It is clear there is no shortage of pastors, theologians, professors, and teachers who feel strongly about how, and how not, to read the Bible. As you can imagine, there is no way in this short book for me to share with you every tool available for reading Scripture. Even so, I would like to give you some guiding principles that will help. Here we go.

Guiding Principle #1: The Holy Spirit Is Your Guide

Before Jesus ascended to heaven, he said some critically revealing things about the Holy Spirit and his role in the believer's life. Here is just a sampling:

Introducing the Bible

> I will ask the Father, and he will send another Companion, who will be with you forever. This Companion is the Spirit of Truth.... You know him, because he lives with you and will be with you.[6]

> The Companion, the Holy Spirit, whom the Father will send in my name, will teach you everything and will remind you of everything I told you.[7]

> When the Companion comes, whom I will send from the Father—the Spirit of Truth who proceeds from the Father—he will testify about me.[8]

> However, when the Spirit of Truth comes, he will guide you in all truth.[9]

If you remember nothing else about how to read the Bible, please make sure this one thing is what you treasure always: the Holy Spirit is your guide through this ancient, beautiful, sometimes mysterious, yet living and powerful story of God called the Bible. It is the Spirit who takes what is ancient and expresses contemporary truth. It is the Spirit who reveals the ancient beauty of Scripture to all cultures and generations. Further, it is the Spirit who takes what is sometimes mysterious in the Bible and brings clarity. Further still, the writer of Hebrews tells us the Bible is living and powerful, sharp, piercing, and discerning of hearts and minds.[10] How can this be? It's just ink on a page, right? Yes, it is certainly ink on paper, but not just ink on paper. What sets the Bible apart from all other books is its author: the Spirit of truth, the Holy Spirit!

Each time you sit to read or listen to the Bible, I encourage you to pray a simple prayer of invitation to the Holy Spirit by way of John 16:13 above to guide you in all truth. And he will!

6. John 14: 16, 17 (CEB).
7. John 14:26 (CEB).
8. John 15:26 (CEB).
9. John 16:13 (CEB).
10. Heb 4:12.

Guiding Principle #2: Always Be On the Lookout for Jesus

Remember in our section on the gospel that Jesus is the central focus of the story of God? No matter where you're reading in the Bible, I encourage you to tune your eyes to look for Jesus. This can be a little tricky while reading the Old Testament since this covers a period of time long before Jesus was born. Even so, remember that there are over three hundred messianic Prophecies in the Old Testament all pointing to Jesus. The more you become familiar with the Bible, the more familiar with these Prophecies you will become.

Further, there are what theologians call types and shadows in the Old Testament. Oooo, sounds spooky and a little dark! Really what they mean by this is that some Old Testament characters act as a type of Christ. For example, some theologians refer to Moses as a type of Christ because he was a rescuer of God's people. Some view King David as a type of Christ because of his priestly reign.

When it comes to shadows, or more precisely foreshadowing, what theologians are referring to here are elements and events in the Old Testament that allude to, or point to, or foreshadow Jesus. A classic example is when the Hebrew people spread the blood of a lamb over their doorposts (Exod 12) so that judgment would "pass over" (remember that annual celebration we mentioned earlier) their household and they would be saved and delivered. In the New Testament, Jesus is referred to as the "Lamb of God" (John 1:29). It was (and is) his blood that is applied to our lives when we say "yes" to following him. In this way, Exod 12 is a foreshadowing of Jesus.

Always be on the lookout for Jesus as you read the Bible.

Guiding Principle #3: First, It *Can* Mean for Us What It Did Mean for Them. Second, Some Things Meant for Them Are *Not* Meant for Us.

Now, a two-parter. This gets into a realm of study called hermeneutics ("herm-uh-noo-tics"). Essentially, the arena of hermeneutics attempts to set up healthy lenses through which we view, examine, study, and apply the Bible. And, depending on who you talk to, there are many. For example, a classic hermeneutic is this: we interpret Scripture with Scripture. This is helpful when we come across a troublesome, or obscure, or seemingly contradictory portion of Scripture. What this hermeneutical lens encourages us to ask is, "What does the rest of the Bible have to say about this, if anything?" As we explore, we may find the Bible has a lot to say elsewhere that helps us interpret this troublesome passage. Or, perhaps we find the Bible has little, if anything, to say about it. In which case, we may be left with a portion of Scripture we have to commit to prayer, trust the Lord to help us with understanding, and perhaps spend some time getting help from our pastor.

The two lenses I put forth here are an attempt to help young Christ-followers not fall into an all-too-common trap I see many Christ-followers fall into: applying Scripture to their lives out of context.

Let's take these one at a time.

First, the Bible *can* mean for us what it did mean for them. Notice the word "can." Implicit here is the idea "not always." Even so, what a gift! The idea of a promise uttered four thousand years ago or two thousand years ago that could apply directly to me is amazing! Let's look at one example from the New Testament, and one from the Old Testament. In the New Testament we find perhaps the most famous of all Scriptures—John 3:16:

> For this is how God loved the world: He gave his one and only Son, so that everyone who believes in him will not perish but have eternal life.[11]

You are part of this world and "everyone" includes you!

And one among many from the Old Testament is found in Gen 12. This is what is known as the Abrahamic covenant. You can read about it in Gen 12, 13, 15, and 17. One small part of the covenant God made with Abraham says this:

---

11. CEB.

All the families on earth will be blessed through you.[12]

Wow, what an amazing promise from God! I have to believe Abraham is thinking, "*Really?* All families on earth will be blessed through me?" I don't know about you, but I want others to be blessed through my life. And to be sure, some have, but not every family on earth!

So how do we know this promise made roughly four thousand years ago applies to us today? Well, we're all blessed by Jesus, his life, death, and resurrection, right? How does this tie to Abraham? The Gospel writer Matthew detailed the family lineage of Jesus and here is how he puts it in the very first verse of the Gospel of Matthew:

> A record of the ancestors of Jesus Christ, son of David, son of Abraham.[13]

Jesus is a descendent of Abraham and a fulfillment of the promise God made to him. The entire world has been blessed through Abraham.

One final distinction: there is a difference between what is beneficial to me, and what is applicable to me. The entire Old Testament, for instance, is beneficial to me, but not all of it should be applied to my life (more on this below). So, not all that is beneficial is applicable, but all that is applicable is beneficial.

Second, some things meant for them are *not* meant for us.

The second way I find folks getting in trouble with reading, understanding, and living out the Bible, is when they attempt to apply something to their own life that is meant for someone else, and not for them. Again, I can benefit from something meant for someone else without unnecessarily applying that something to my life. Let me illustrate this a couple of ways.

First, I enjoy reading the stories, biographies, and memoirs of historical figures. Their stories are often moving, inspiring, and challenging. I benefit in these ways from reading their stories. I

---

12. Gen 12:3(b) (CEB).
13. Matt 1:1 (CEB).

may even benefit by applying some principles from their lives to my own. However, I don't make the mistake of attempting to superimpose their lives, settings, and actions over my own life. In fact, to do so may wind up hurting me and those around me. Some of what was meant for them is not meant for me.

Second, let's look at one example from the Bible among at least hundreds. If we return to the Abrahamic covenant mentioned above, we agreed that it applies to us today in that we are certainly blessed through the covenant made by God to Abraham. However, God chose to ratify the covenant through circumcision of the Hebrew people. It became the mark, or the sign, of God's covenant to Abraham. This now poses a question: "Do I need to be circumcised since the covenant applies to me?" Great question, and the answer is "no." Look here at what the apostle Paul says in Galatians:

> Look, I, Paul, am telling you that if you have yourselves circumcised, having Christ won't help you. . . . Being circumcised or not being circumcised doesn't matter in Christ Jesus, but faith working through love does matter.[14]

Paul tells the churches in the ancient region of Galatia (area of modern-day Turkey) that the blessing they are receiving from being included in the Abrahamic covenant is applied to their life not through circumcision, but rather by God's grace through faith by the Christ-follower.

Some things meant for them are not meant for us.

Guiding Principle #4: The Bible Becomes a Mirror for Our Own Soul

There are days when I'm thankful for the mirrors in my home, and other days not so much. Passing in front of a mirror in the morning when I look like I've just come out of my dryer's spin cycle, bags under my eyes, dried saliva on one side of my face, both eye and nose boogers glaring at me, as well as several extra pounds

14. Gal 5:2, 6 (CEB).

relaxing around my waist . . . doesn't engender warm, fuzzy feelings toward my mirrors.

However, when I try on a new shirt, or need to straighten a tie, or get a better look at a wound, or simply gaze at my wife's reflection . . . on those days I'm thankful for the mirrors in my home.

Even so, I keep mirrors in my house because I need to see both the good and the bad. On the bad days, how would I know to straighten and remove things if I couldn't see it reflected back to me? Likewise, how would I know if my appearance is hitting the mark if I couldn't see it reflected back to me?

So it is with the Bible. As we read, it becomes a mirror for our soul, our actions, and our life. When I think about the repeated rebellion of the children of Israel turning their backs on God, and just when I find myself shaking my head at their hard hearts, stubbornness, and faithlessness, my own rebellion and faithlessness toward God is reflected back to me. Or when the Proverbs declare this: "Fools show all their anger, but the wise hold it back,"[15] my first response is to apply this verse to my boss, weird uncle, my two-year-old, or coworker who snapped at me, but when I remember that the Bible is a mirror to my own soul, I'm able to reflect on all the ways I've given vent to my own anger.

Friend, the Bible does not shy away from telling the stories of some really messed up people! Murderers, thieves, prostitutes, adulterers, the arrogant, the hypocritical, the faithless, the fearful and more are all part of the story of God. Further, many of these folks are God-following, Christ-loving believers! In their story, I often find my own. Before we shake our heads at their sin and misgivings, we first need to take a long look at what is being reflected back to us by the mirror of their story.

Guiding Principle #5: Be Consistent

As God was reconstructing, rebuilding, and reshaping the Hebrew people into a whole new community after being enslaved for four

---

15. Prov 29:11 (CEB).

hundred years, one of the lessons he wove into their consciences was their daily need for, and dependance on, God. Not only did they need God's help with protection and direction, but even for their daily sustenance.

One of the ways God chose to illustrate this lesson was through their food procurement and intake. Remember, they were slaves for four hundred years. They were given food by their captors and told when, where, and how to eat. They didn't hunt or gather their own food.

Now God had delivered them from Pharaoh's hand and led them into the Sinai desert wilderness. Now what? How in the world were they going to feed themselves? God chose to provide them with quail, and something called manna (Exod 16). What is interesting is that he told them not to stock up or hoard the food he was providing, but rather to only gather what was needed for their families for that day.

As you'll read in Exod 16, some decided to push the boundaries of this instruction and gathered more than their daily need. It was full of maggots by morning. What's the point? I want to suggest that God was reinforcing the idea in the hearts of his people that they needed him not just once per week, or month, or year, or when they were being attacked, or had a math test, or job interview, or were short on their monthly bills—they needed God every day. And so it is with me, and so it is with you. We need God every day.

Jesus said this in Matt 4:4: "It's written, *People won't live only by bread, but by every word spoken by God.*"[16] As we outlined earlier in this chapter, the Bible is the story of God, told by God using the agency of human beings to record it. It is the written word of God and is one way we can receive daily "manna" from him.

---

16. CEB (emphasis original).

Guiding Principle #6: Check with Your Pastor on Some Bible Reading Methods, Plans, and Tools—There Are Many!

It is yet another reason to plug into a local church in your area, if you haven't already. The pastors and leaders in that church can help equip you with tools to engage the Bible consistently and wisely.

Even so, I've provided a few resources in the appendix to get you started.

Chapter 3 Discussion Questions:

1. Have you ever tried to read the Bible? Was it difficult? Easy?
2. Have you ever considered that the Bible is simply the story of God?
3. Have you found a translation of the Bible that is a good fit for you? If not, was this chapter a helpful guide? How so?
4. As you review this chapter and the resources outlined in the appendix, what is one small step you can take to begin the journey of incorporating the Bible into your life each day?

4

Introducing Faith
Belief vs. Trust

"To believe certain facts about who Christ is and what he has done for us is a vital first state, but true faith must turn such mental belief into a decisive act of trust. Intellectual conviction must lead to personal commitment."[1]

IT IS LIKELY YOU were gifted this book or purchased it because you've shifted your weight from unbelief in Jesus, to belief in Jesus. Somehow, as I mentioned in the "Who is this book for?" section of the Introduction, you have confessed your faith in Jesus. I want you to notice a few words already used in this chapter: "belief," "unbelief," "confessed," and "faith." Why would I highlight these words?

Here's why: take a look at what the apostle Paul says in Romans:

> Because if you confess with your mouth "Jesus is Lord" and in your heart you have faith that God raised him from the dead, you will be saved. Trusting with the heart

---

1. Stott, *Basic Christianity*, 125.

leads to righteousness, and confessing with the mouth leads to salvation.[2]

Or, more simply put from the mouths of Paul and Silas when responding to one of their jailers who asked what he needed to do to be saved:

> They replied, "Believe in the Lord Jesus, and you will be saved."[3]

I'm taking the time to cover this because it's a big deal! If you confessed with your mouth your belief in Jesus and desire to follow him—then according to the verses above, you're saved!

While that is true, there is something else equally true. Jesus didn't just invite people to believe in him, he also invited them to follow him. I want to suggest that this is the difference between *confessional* belief and *convictional* belief.

In his book *The King Jesus Gospel*, author Scot McKnight makes the case that the gospel of Jesus Christ is not only people raising their hand, or praying a prayer—it is about discipleship.[4]

Let me illustrate this idea of confessional belief (faith expressed with words) vs. convictional belief (faith expressed with behavior) using another tightrope story. Long before Philippe Petit was born, another tightrope walker named Charles Blondin decided to tightrope walk from the United States to Canada . . . suspended over Niagara Falls!

In 1859, Mr. Blondin tied a rope 1,100 feet long and suspended it 160 feet over the falls with no safety net. He charged a nickel to anyone who wanted to watch and, to the amazement and cheers of the crowd of nearly 25,000 on June 30, 1859, he made it safely from the US to Canada and back.

In the ensuing years, it is estimated that Blondin crossed Niagara Falls roughly three hundred times, each trip increasing in difficulty and risk. It is reported he once walked backward to

---

2. Rom 10:9–10 (CEB).
3. Acts 16:31 (CEB).
4. The word "disciple" in the New Testament means "learner" and "follower" of Jesus Christ.

Introducing Faith

Canada; he carried his agent piggyback-style over and back; he once crossed while incorporating somersaults and backflips; and, perhaps most famously on one occasion, he hauled a stove out to the center of the tightrope, made a fire, and cooked an omelet!

However, one of his stunts especially stands out to me. One day Blondin showed up with a wheelbarrow, loaded it with several hundred pounds of weight, and crossed from one side to the other. He then asked the cheering, wide-eyed crowd whether they thought he could successfully carry a person in the wheelbarrow. Of course, they all cheered in agreement. Blondin then isolated one man and entered this dialogue with him:

> Blondin: "Do you think I could safely carry you across in the wheelbarrow?"
> The man: "Yes, of course."
> Blondin: "Get in," Blondin said with a smile.
> The man declined.

You see, the man had a confessional belief (words) that Blondin could accomplish the stunt, but he didn't have a convictional belief (action/behavior) that he could.

Jesus calls us to both. Back to Jesus' sibling, James, who wrote concerning this very topic:

> Someone might claim, "You have faith and I have action." But how can I see your faith apart from your actions? Instead, I'll show you my faith by putting it into practice in faithful action.[5]

I encourage you to get in the wheelbarrow my friend.

CHAPTER 4 DISCUSSION QUESTIONS:

1. What comes to mind when you think about the idea of confessional belief in Jesus vs. convictional belief in Jesus?
2. What is one way you can put your faith into action this week?

---

5. Jas 2:18 (CEB).

5

Introducing the Goal
Look in the Mirror

"The image of Christ is the fulfillment of the deepest hungers of the human heart for wholeness."[1]

ONE OF MY FAVORITE authors is Robert Mulholland. He taught at Asbury Theological Seminary and created several key resources to help Christ-followers understand spiritual formation. One of his books, *Invitation to a Journey: A Road Map for Spiritual Formation*, has been especially formational in my life. He offers this as a working definition for spiritual formation: "Spiritual formation is a process of being conformed to the image of Christ for the sake of others."[2]

Dr. Mulholland makes the case that "the process of spiritual shaping is a primal reality of human existence. Everyone is in a process of spiritual formation!"[3] He drives this point home with this sobering thought: "We are being shaped into either the

---

1. Mulholland Jr., *Invitation to a Journey*, 34.
2. Mulholland Jr., *Invitation to a Journey*, 12.
3. Mulholland Jr., *Invitation to a Journey*, 23.

Introducing the Goal

wholeness of the image of Christ or a horribly destructive caricature of that image—destructive not only to ourselves but also to others, for we inflict our brokenness upon them."[4]

If this is true, then each step you take on your journey of life is rooted in being spiritually formed one way or another. So then, it might be good to know what the goal is as you walk with Jesus.

I want to suggest the goal is that the reflection in the mirror each day looks more and more like Jesus. Not our exterior looks of course, but the nature of our interior life measured by our thoughts and actions. Is our life, for instance, producing the fruit of the Holy Spirit outlined in Gal 5: love, joy, peace, patience, kindness, goodness, faithfulness, gentleness, and self-control? Or, are we producing what the apostle Paul refers to as the "works of the flesh" outlined in the same portion of Gal 5?

The whole goal of your next step, and every step thereafter, is to be conformed to the image of Christ, but to what end? For the sake of other people. God created you to be in relationship both with himself and others. We are created for relationship!

I can almost hear a collective "hallelujah" from my extroverted friends, and a groan from all my fellow introverted friends. I'm solidly in the latter camp. People can be messy, and time-consuming. However, when I look in the mirror, I find that I'm one of them! Further, those same messy, time-consuming people are ones Christ loves and died for.

Here is something I know about both extroverted and introverted camps—you love people! Your extroverted or introverted nature simply speaks to how you recharge, either with people or away from them. This does not change the fact that we are relational creatures.

Our wholeness in Christ takes place in the midst of our relationship with others, not apart from them.[5] As we grow in Christ, we begin to reflect his grace, kindness, patience, and encouragement to those around us.

---

4. Mulholland Jr., *Invitation to a Journey*, 23.
5. Mulholland Jr., *Invitation to a Journey*, 42.

If you ever lose sight of the goal of your Christian walk, just look in the mirror as a reminder. Is your interior life—your thoughts and actions—looking more and more like Jesus? And how is it translating through your actions to impact those around you?

Chapter 5 Discussion Questions:

1. Have you ever considered that everyone is in the process of spiritual formation—either becoming more like Jesus or a marred image of Jesus?
2. When you think about Jesus at work in your life conforming you into his image, what thoughts come to your mind?
3. One thing not mentioned here about Dr. Mulholland is that he suggests Jesus will often start at the point in our lives where we are most dissimilar to his image. If you feel comfortable, write down or share the area of your life that seems most dissimilar to the image of Christ.

6

Introducing Some Potential Next Steps

"Shall I ever-so-slightly shift my weight to the left, my right leg will be unburdened, my right foot will freely meet the wire."—Philippe Petit

I WANT TO END our time together by offering a few potential next steps. You have already taken at least two critical ones: you shifted your weight from unbelief to belief in Christ, and you've read this far in the book! What will be your next steps along the high wire of faith? Here are a few to consider.

A Step Toward Community: God's People

Throughout our time together, I've encouraged you to get connected with a local church in your area if you haven't already. Why? Great question. Let me briefly outline a few reasons why it is important for Christ-followers to connect to a local church. First, we probably should define what the church is and is not.

The Greek word for "church" in the New Testament is "ekklēsia." It's a powerful little word that simply means "a gathered people." Notice, church does not mean "building" or "institution." The church of Jesus Christ is people!

Now, a few reasons I would encourage you to become part of this "gathered people":

1. The church is the foundation of truth on the earth.

> I am writing these things to you now, even though I hope to be with you soon, so that if I am delayed, you will know how people must conduct themselves in the household of God. This is the church of the living God, which is the pillar and foundation of the truth.[1]

In a culture of shifting relativism, the Spirit maintains his anchor of truth in and through the local church.

2. Christ loves his church and is committed to her!

> Christ loved the church and gave himself up for her . . . and to present her to himself as a radiant church, without stain or wrinkle or any other blemish, but holy and blameless.[2]

The church has the privilege of being described as the bride and body of Christ—his hands, his feet, his heart (1 Cor 12:12–31). Ephesians 5 above makes it clear the beautiful work of change God is doing in his people, he is doing through the local church.

3. Becoming part of a local church is an antidote to the fear of commitment.

We live in a time where it seems commitment outside of self is at a premium. Commitment to a friend, family, marriage, a job, the broken margins of community, seem to be more the exception than the rule. This orientation of heart has produced, in part, a generation of "church shoppers and hoppers" untethered from commitment. Planting yourself and committing to a local church swims against the tide of American consumerism and fickleness.

1. 1 Tim 3:14 (NLT).
2. Eph 5:25, 27 (NIV).

Introducing Some Potential Next Steps

It is an unselfish decision to commit to a local church. Commitment always builds character and is a tool God uses to shape us more and more into his image.

4. It will help produce spiritual growth.

The New Testament places a major emphasis on the need for Christ-followers to be accountable to one another for spiritual growth. The main apparatus Christ provided for this growth is the local church. In fact, the New Testament outlines at least thirty-four of what are called "one-anotherings." Love one another (John 13:34), be devoted to one another, honor one another (Rom 12:10), live in harmony with one another (Rom 12:16), teach one another, admonish one another (Col 3:16), comfort one another (1 Thess 4:18), and many more! All of these are meant to build up the church and to produce spiritual growth.

5. It helps meet one of humanity's greatest needs.

Isolating ourselves is one of the greatest mistakes we can make, and the journey toward making the decision to do so generally goes something like this . . .

> Our greatest need: To be known, which leads to . . .
> Our greatest fear: If you really knew me you wouldn't love me, which leads to . . .
> Our greatest pain: Rejection, which leads to . . .
> Our greatest mistake: Isolation.

Christ provided the antidote to this: a local church willing to commit to one another, love one another, and pray for one another along the journey.

How Do I Find a Church?

Another great question. I'll admit, sometimes this can be difficult. I would encourage you with a few simple steps:

1. Pray and ask the Holy Spirit to guide you.
2. Ask the person who gave you this book to help you find a church.
3. Don't get discouraged in your search. Churches come in all shapes and sizes, and not all of them will fit you, but one will! Keep at it.
4. Once you find the church where you sense the Holy Spirit has led you, make a commitment to that gathered group of people. Don't just attend, but rather attach to the community of faith. The next few steps I outline below are ways to do just this: attach.

A Step Toward Baptism: God's Mark

What is baptism, and why would I encourage you to make this one of your next steps? I'm glad you asked. Please note that there may be some churches who disagree at some level with what I outline below. Don't be alarmed by that. I would encourage you to listen to them and walk through the process they outline.

First, let's start with "why." Two main reasons I would encourage you to be baptized are that (a) Jesus commanded it (Matt 28:19), and (b) Jesus modeled it (Matt 3:15–17). What an amazing thought that God himself was baptized!

Second, what is baptism? Over the years I've taught baptism candidates that baptism is "an outward sign of an inward commitment." The inward commitment is our choice to place our faith in Jesus. I often illustrate this principle by referring to baptism as "the wedding ring of salvation." I wear a wedding ring on my finger as an outward symbol of an inward commitment I've made to my wife, Joy. The ring serves to remind me and others of the commitment I've made to her.

Last, baptism represents a powerful truth: in baptism, we identify with Jesus in his death, burial, and resurrection. Listen to what the apostle Paul says here:

Introducing Some Potential Next Steps

> Therefore, if anyone is in Christ, he is a new creation. The old has passed away; behold, the new has come.[3]

Let me now add some notes in parenthesis to this verse just to help you see the powerful picture of baptism:

> Therefore, if anyone is in Christ, he is a new creation. The old has passed away (the old, sinful person symbolically buried under the water); behold, the new has come (coming up out of the water, rising to new life in Christ!).[4]

Make sure to ask one of the pastors at your church when the next opportunity to be baptized is and what your church's process is.

A Step Toward Bible Reading: God's Wisdom

> "Blessed is the one who finds wisdom, and the one who gets understanding, for the gain from her is better than gain from silver and her profit better than gold. She is more precious than jewels, and nothing you desire can compare with her."[5]

We spent an entire chapter talking about what the Bible is, some basics on how to read it, even what version(s) one should consider reading and why. There is no need to cover this again here, except to encourage you to get your hands on a Bible (hard copy or digital) and begin the discipline of daily digesting the story of God found within its pages. In it, you will find encouragement, correction, direction, and the priceless wisdom of God!

Again, I've provided some helpful resources to get you started in the appendix.

---

3. 2 Cor 5:17 (ESV).
4. 2 Cor 5:17 (ESV; parentheses and commentary added).
5. Prov 3:13–15 (ESV).

A Step Toward Prayer: God's Communication

> "God warms his hands at man's heart when he prays."[6]

> "The Lord's eyes are on the righteous and his ears are open to their prayers."[7]

I'm probably the last person who should be writing anything about prayer. I received a "C" in prayer when I was in seminary. True story. It seems to me there are just certain subjects a pastor should be able to score at least a solid "B" or higher on, and prayer is one of them. Oh well, you can add me to your prayer list.

When I was a kid, I learned what I've now come to refer to as "The Grim Reaper" prayer. See if you recognize it; it goes something like this:

"Now I lay me down to sleep, / I pray the Lord my soul to keep. / And if I die, before I wake, / I pray the Lord my soul to take."

Whoever penned this prayer needs to repent for the untold thousands of little anxiety-ridden insomniacs it created. *Who teaches a kid to pray like this?* (In my case, it was my older sister). *And if I die before I wake, I pray the Lord my soul to take?* Perhaps the only good that came of the prayer is that it scared the fires of hell right out of me.

What Is Christian Prayer?

Let's start with a working definition of Christian prayer. I use the phrase "Christian prayer" because I'm aware there are many kinds of prayer among the world religions. Here we go:

> Christian prayer is an act of faith by the Christ-follower. It is a dialogue (not always with words) between the Christ-follower and the triune (three-in-one) God of the Bible.

---

6. This quote is often attributed to John Masefield; however, its true origin seems to be unknown.

7. 1 Pet 3:12 (CEB).

Introducing Some Potential Next Steps

Please take note of a few words—"act of faith," "dialogue" (not always with words), and "triune God." Let's briefly take them one at a time.

Act of Faith

The very nature of prayer is an act of faith. Sometimes I will have people remark to me that they're not sure "if they have the gift of faith," or "whether they have enough faith," or wish they "could have more faith." One of the things I tune into with them is whether they have an active prayer life. If they are praying, they are exercising faith! Why? Because the very act of prayer is a declaration: "I cannot do this on my own, I need help." And, I'm choosing to pray to a God I can't see like I see my friend, or hear like I hear my friend. It is an act of humility, an act of trust, and an act of faith.

Dialogue

There is this incredible story in the Old Testament of a young man named Daniel. He was a Hebrew, and his people had been captured by the Babylonians under a king named Nebuchadnezzar (probably made fun of for his name in high school . . . just saying). Daniel is arguably most famous for a death sentence he was given: death by lion (Dan 6). He was gifted, wise, faithful, and had a robust prayer life. In fact, the reason he was thrown to the lions was because of his prayer life. However, here is a separate story related to one of his prayer times. Take a look:

> Then the man said to me, "Don't be afraid, Daniel, because from the day you first set your mind to understand things and to humble yourself before your God, your words were heard. I've come because of your words! For twenty-one days the leader of the Persian kingdom blocked my way. But then Michael, one of the highest leaders, came to help me. I left Michael there with the leader of the Persian kingdom.[8]

8. Dan 10:12–13 (CEB).

Notice there was someone "on the other end of the line," that Daniel's prayers were heard, and, not only that, there was also a response from God! Prayer is a dialogue.

If we go to the New Testament, we find another incredible story. There is a priest named Zechariah, and the Bible says that he and his wife are "blameless in their observance of all the Lord's commandments and regulations."[9] One day he is in the temple performing his priestly duties and an angel shows up:

> The angel said, "Don't be afraid, Zechariah. Your prayers have been heard."[10]

Again, not only are Zechariah's prayers heard, but God responds. Now, you might be asking, "Does this mean an angel in some human form is going to show up when I pray?" I suppose this could happen, but not likely. What I do want to embed deep in your heart is that God hears you when you pray, and his heart is a two-way communication. His response may not be in your timing, or even in a way you might expect. We find in Scripture that God speaks to his people in a myriad of ways: dreams, visions, angelic messengers, through people, through the written words of the Bible, and through the voice of the Holy Spirit, to name a few.

I think you will find the most consistent ways God speaks to us today is (a) through the Bible, (b) through the promptings and voice of the Holy Spirit, and (c) through other Christ-followers.

Triune God

Remember my brilliant-minded engineer asking who he should pray to: God, Jesus, or the Holy Spirit? You'll recall my answer to him was "yes."

Friends, remember God is God, Jesus is God, and the Holy Spirit is God. You can address your prayer to any one of them, or all three! I want to encourage you not to overthink this. God hears you. Jesus hears you. The Holy Spirit hears you.

9. Luke 1:6 (CEB).
10. Luke 1:13 (CEB).

Introducing Some Potential Next Steps

Why Should I Pray?

Much like baptism, Jesus modeled prayer. Imagine that. Jesus very often prayed to God the Father. In fact, his life was one of prayer. He often prayed alone, he prayed for people, he prayed over meals, he taught prayer, and he even prayed for you! (Take a look at John 17 sometime.) If the goal is to be conformed into Christ's image, then our lives must become lives of prayer.

Second, Jesus and our New Testament invites us to—even presumes that we will—pray. Look here at what the apostle Paul says:

> Don't be anxious about anything; rather, bring up all of your requests to God in your prayers and petitions, along with giving thanks.[11]

And from the mouth of Jesus:

> When you pray, don't be like hypocrites. . . . But when you pray, go to your room, shut the door, and pray to your Father who is present in that secret place. . . . When you pray, don't pour out a flood of empty words, as the Gentiles do. They think that by saying many words they'll be heard. Don't be like them, because your Father knows what you need before you ask.[12]

Third, when we pray it develops our relationship with God. Do me a favor and think of either your best friend or spouse, or both. Now, let me ask you: would you have any relationship with them without communication? Of course not. However, as you build healthy rhythms of communication, your relationship grows. So it is with God.

Fourth, prayer invites the presence of God. Remember Daniel and Zechariah, previously mentioned? Both their lives of prayer garnered the presence of heaven. Or, how about something Jesus tucked into a teaching about relationships, reconciliation, and forgiveness:

---

11. Phil 4:6 (CEB).
12. Matt 6:5, 6, 7 (CEB).

> Take this most seriously: A yes on earth is yes in heaven; a no on earth is no in heaven. What you say to one another is eternal. I mean this. When two of you get together on anything at all on earth and make a prayer of it, my Father in heaven goes into action. And when two or three of you are together because of me, you can be sure that I'll be there.[13]

Fifth, when we pray, we experience the peace of God. Let's go back to the Phil 4:6 verse above and add verse 7 for fuller context. The first part goes like this:

> Don't be anxious about anything; rather, bring up all of your requests to God in your prayers and petitions, along with giving thanks.[14]

And here is the result:

> Then the peace of God that exceeds all understanding will keep your hearts and minds safe in Christ Jesus.[15]

Last, we gain the wisdom and perspective of God. Isn't this what we want? Again, the very act of prayer makes a clear statement: "I can't do this on my own, I need God and his wisdom and direction!"

Look at what James, the half brother of Jesus, said about how we receive wisdom:

> But anyone who needs wisdom should ask God, whose very nature is to give to everyone without a second thought, without keeping score.[16]

Friend, I could go on. The benefit, blessing, and power of prayer are immense!

---

13. Matt 18:18–20 (MSG).
14. Phil 4:6 (CEB).
15. Phil 4:7 (CEB).
16. Jas 1:5 (CEB).

Introducing Some Potential Next Steps

How Should I Pray?

Though I added a "C" to my transcripts in prayer, I did learn a few things— not least is that there are all kinds of prayers: silent prayer, breath prayer, form prayer, individual prayer, corporate prayer, supplication prayer, declarative prayer, and many more. What I want you to understand is that there is no one way to pray. Each one of these is *a* way to pray, not *the* way to pray.

What is interesting about this question—"How should I pray?"—is that it's the very question the disciples asked Jesus. Look here:

> Jesus was praying in a certain place. When he finished, one of his disciples said, "Lord, teach us to pray, just as John taught his disciples."[17]

They wanted to know how to pray and so Jesus taught them how to pray. He gave them a framework for prayer that was simple, direct, humble, and God-honoring. You can read what he taught them in Luke 11:1-4. Since it would be silly for me to attempt to build on what Jesus has already taught, I might offer three considerations as you begin your life of prayer:

Keep It Real

I want to take you back to Matt 6:5 to review what Jesus taught about prayer. Again, the context is what is referred to as the Sermon on the Mount (because Jesus decided to go up on a mountain to teach). It's a sermon that included a wide range of topics—ingredients to happiness, murder, adultery, divorce, retaliation, judging others, forgiveness, generosity, fasting, prayer, and more. You can read the entire sermon in Matt 5-7. In chapter 6, Jesus is addressing the idea of making a show of our spirituality—showy generosity, showy prayer, and showy fasting. Here is what he says about attempting to showboat with one's prayer life:

---

17. Luke 11:1 (CEB).

> When you pray, don't be like hypocrites. They love to pray standing in the synagogues and on the street corners so that people will see them. I assure you, that's the only reward they'll get. But when you pray, go to your room, shut the door, and pray to your Father who is present in that secret place. Your Father who sees what you do in secret will reward you. When you pray, don't pour out a flood of empty words, as the Gentiles do. They think that by saying many words they'll be heard. Don't be like them, because your Father knows what you need before you ask.[18]

Friends, keep your prayer real and authentic. Share with God what is on your heart and mind. Share with him where you need help, and where you're struggling. Jesus invites us to simply be ourselves when we pray.

Keep It Simple

In the team's first spring practice of 1961, famed NFL football coach Vince Lombardi stood in front of his Green Bay Packer players. They had suffered a crushing loss the previous season in the NFL Championship game to the Philadelphia Eagles. He picked up a football and said, "Gentlemen, this is a football." Can you imagine? These are professional athletes at the top of their game who had just been to a championship game! As the legendary story goes, he had them sit down on the grass and open their team playbook to page one where they were reintroduced to the game's fundamentals of blocking, tackling, and catching.

Coach Lombardi's focus on simplicity, the basics, and fundamentals paid off as they won the NFL Championship that season 37–0 against the New York Giants. He never coached a team with a losing season after that and never lost a playoff game again.

My friend's oldest son is named Nicholas. When he was younger, around four or five years old, he could not abide long-winded prayers. I remember babysitting him and there were

---

18. Matt 6:5–8 (CEB).

Introducing Some Potential Next Steps

multiple times he would interrupt the prayer before dinner with a loud "Amen!" if it lasted any more than about ten seconds!

It seems to me that Nicholas and Jesus are of the same mindset—keep the prayer simple. Listen again to verse 7 above:

> When you pray, don't pour out a flood of empty words, as the Gentiles do. They think that by saying many words they'll be heard. Don't be like them.[19]

Hopefully this is a pressure reliever for you. You don't have to come up with a bunch of fancy words and present them in some fancy way; rather you are exhorted by Jesus to keep it real, and keep it simple. Why? "Because your Father knows what you need before you ask."[20]

Keep It Consistent

Let's go back to the analogy of your best friend or spouse I mentioned earlier. What would happen if you spoke with your spouse only once or twice a year? Some of you may be thinking, "I have, and it hasn't gone too well." Exactly. Or, what if you communicated only when you needed something? It wouldn't work. So it is with our communication (prayer) with God. It says this in 1 Thess 5:17: "Pray continually."

You might be thinking, "How in the world can anyone actually do that? We have to sleep sometime, right?" Correct. There is no way even practically that the most spiritual person could pray continually. Even Jesus, when he walked the earth, didn't pray 24/7. So, there must be something else to this word "continually"—which there is.

Different translations of the Bible use different words here: "without ceasing" (ESV), "unceasing and persistent" (AMP), "never stop" (NLT). At the core of this word in the original Greek

---

19. Matt 6:7 (CEB).
20. Matt 6:8(b) (CEB).

language is this meaning: constantly, unceasingly by an unvarying practice.[21]

Ah, the apostle Paul has our habits and practices in mind. Could we, as Christ-followers, build such a practiced rhythm of prayer into our lives that it is as if we're praying continually? Let me illustrate.

I have a friend named Caleb and his default response to any need or crisis is, "Let's pray and ask God . . ." It is as if he's praying continually because he has made prayer an unvarying practice in his life.

The benefits and power of prayer are immeasurable. Keep it real, keep it simple, and keep it consistent.

A Step Toward Serving: God's Help

About a year ago, we had an ice storm in our area that effectively shut down the city. It was the perfect evening: the Green Bay Packers (I forgot to mention, my favorite team!) were ahead in their Wild Card playoff game. Joy and I were doing a quasi-online "watch party" of the game with our adult kids, and we had some carne asada marinading, ready to be cooked into a celebratory meal as a Packer win seemed inevitable. It was white and wintery outside, and warm, cozy, and joyful inside. A piece of heaven on earth.

With the game well in hand, I decided to get up and start making dinner. I decided to start chopping up the toppings for our tacos: lettuce, tomato, olives, cheese, and the like. As I was chopping the lettuce, I had one eye on the game, and one eye on my mad culinary skills, along with excitement for yet another Packer win pulsing through my veins. At one point, while glancing at the game, I heard a crunch that didn't sound like lettuce, and certainly didn't feel like lettuce. When I looked down, the lettuce was no longer green but red. I had chopped the tip of my index finger off at an angle.

---

21. StepBible.org, "1 Thessalonians 5."

Introducing Some Potential Next Steps

As I was hovering over the kitchen sink growing pale in the face, I let Joy know I had cut my finger badly. Joy is calm and cool under pressure. You could say I'm the opposite. She took a quick look. "Oh yeah, you did. Let's have Kayla take a look." Our daughter, Kayla, is a nurse and was on our FaceTime watch party. I stumbled over to my computer and removed the compression wrap of paper towels I had a death grip on. As soon as I removed the wrap blood poured all over my computer. Now what? We knew I needed an emergency room, but the city was all but shut down because of the inches-thick sheet of ice covering it, and we didn't have a four-wheel-drive vehicle or snow tires. We called a local urgent care and they let us know they would be closing in thirty minutes. Our son came in his Suburban, picked up his genius chef dad to make the dangerous trek to urgent care. Ninety minutes later, with a finger tourniquet, a few shots to numb the pain, a good cleaning of the wound, some surgical foam, and some antibiotics, color began to return to my face.

This is one of many stories I could share of bumps, bruises, stitches, broken bones, and casts I've had in my illustrious life of safe living. In fact, when I was younger, I broke my femur and was in a plaster body cast for a couple of months and had to learn to walk again after it was removed. What I'm trying to say is that I understand what it means to have certain parts of my body not working at full capacity, if at all.

In the apostle Paul's first letter to the church at Corinth, he is instructing them about spiritual gifts, and the importance of using them to serve one another. Take a look at what he says:

> Christ is just like the human body—a body is a unit and has many parts; and all the parts of the body are one body, even though there are many. We were all baptized by one Spirit into one body, whether Jew or Greek, or slave or free, and we all were given one Spirit to drink. Certainly the body isn't one part but many. If the foot says, "I'm not part of the body because I'm not a hand," does that mean it's not part of the body? If the ear says, "I'm not part of the body because I'm not an eye," does that mean it's not part of the body? If the whole body were an eye, what

would happen to the hearing? And if the whole body were an ear, what would happen to the sense of smell? But as it is, God has placed each one of the parts in the body just like he wanted. If all were one and the same body part, what would happen to the body? But as it is, there are many parts but one body. So the eye can't say to the hand, "I don't need you," or in turn, the head can't say to the feet, "I don't need you." Instead, the parts of the body that people think are the weakest are the most necessary. The parts of the body that we think are less honorable are the ones we honor the most. The private parts of our body that aren't presentable are the ones that are given the most dignity. The parts of our body that are presentable don't need this. But God has put the body together, giving greater honor to the part with less honor so that there won't be division in the body and so the parts might have mutual concern for each other. If one part suffers, all the parts suffer with it; if one part gets the glory, all the parts celebrate with it. You are the body of Christ and parts of each other.[22]

Listen to the same apostle Paul in his letter to the Ephesian church:

> God put everything under Christ's feet and made him head of everything in the church, which is his body. His body, the church, is the fullness of Christ, who fills everything in every way.[23]

In fact, just to drill down a little more on this idea of the church being described metaphorically as Christ's body, listen to the same verse in The Message version of the Bible:

> He is in charge of it all, has the final word on everything. At the center of all this, Christ rules the church. The church, you see, is not peripheral to the world; the world is peripheral to the church. The church is Christ's body, in which he speaks and acts, by which he fills everything with his presence.[24]

---

22. 1 Cor 12:12–27 (CEB).
23. Eph 1:22–23 (CEB).
24. Eph 1:22–23 (MSG).

Introducing Some Potential Next Steps

Friend, let's put all this together. Jesus is in charge! His body is the church made up of this beautiful landscape of people from every tribe, tongue, color, culture, skill set, personality, spiritual gift mix, and more. Further, Paul says that we are the church, and members of one another. Beautiful unity (one body), and beautiful diversity (gifts, talents, personalities, cultures), all at once!

You are part of Christ's body and you are needed! As I found out with my missing fingertip and many other bodily injuries, my body suffers and doesn't function quite right with part of it out of commission. So it is with the body of Christ. Notice Paul says, "If one part suffers, all the parts suffer with it."

So, what do we do? Answer: use your God-given personality, strengths, and spiritual gifts to serve the body of Christ. Now, you may know your personality type and what your strengths are, especially if you've taken any type of personality inventory or strengths inventory like "StrengthsFinder." However, you may not fully understand what spiritual gifts are. Let me give you a working definition:

> Spiritual gifts are special divine empowerments given to each believer by the Holy Spirit to accomplish your God-given purpose, with the help of the Holy Spirit, to be used within the context of the body of Christ and/or for the sake of others.

Notice, these are gifts given to each Christ-follower (including you!) for the purpose of serving other people (1 Pet 4:10). So, what are some examples of spiritual gifts outlined in the Bible? What follows is not an exhaustive list, but it will give you a taste:

- Evangelism (Eph 4:11)
- Pastor (Eph 4:11)
- Teaching (Eph 4:11)
- Administration (1 Cor 12:28)
- Encouragement (Rom 12:8)
- Leadership (Rom 12:8)
- Giving (Rom 12:8)
- Discernment (1 Cor 12:10)
- Knowledge (1 Cor 12:8)
- Wisdom (1 Cor 12:8)
- Prophesy (Rom 12:6; 1 Cor 12:10)
- Healing (1 Cor 12:9)

I want to note that each of these gifts the Holy Spirit gives to people in the church will look as varied as the people within the church! Let's take the spiritual gift of encouragement. *Can you imagine how many different ways this might look based on how many Christ-followers there are in the world?* Or, how about the spiritual gift of teaching? You may attend a church that has multiple people who teach the Bible, but do they all teach the same way? Of course not, but they all possess the spiritual gift of teaching.

Whether it's working with kids, youth, young adults, the elderly, the infirmed, the incarcerated, greeting, serving coffee, teaching, encouraging, administrating, leading, or cleaning toilets, I encourage you to have a conversation with one of the leaders or pastors at your church to find out how you can begin to serve the body of Christ.

Introducing Some Potential Next Steps

A Step Toward Generosity: God's Provision

"One can give without loving, but one cannot love without giving."—author unknown[25]

See if you can finish this sentence: "I don't like attending church because all they talk about is . . ." Or, maybe a little variation: "I don't like going to church because all they want from me is my . . ."

If you answered "money," you got it. There may be other ways people finish this sentence, but this is the one I've heard the most over the years.

And, let's be honest, the church worldwide is not immune to scandal. In fact, she has been rocked by very public financial scandals throughout her history. Perhaps you've heard of or been part of a church where there was a mismanagement or abuse of finances. Just a few years back, the pastors within one of the organizations I'm affiliated with received notification that one of the employees of the organization had embezzled over $200,000 spanning a ten-year period. In fact, the money stolen was given by pastors! Ouch.

Of all the portions of this book I've agonized over, read, re-read, and rewritten, it's this one, in large part because of what I've just outlined in the first few sentences of this section.

Even so, I have discovered three main reasons why Christ-followers tend not to be generous—specifically with money. First, they simply do not know what Scripture has to say about money, especially if they are new to following Jesus—how could they? Second, they're deep in debt and have a difficult time justifying giving a portion of their income away while trying to claw out of a hole. Last, if they're honest, they simply do not trust God to take care of their needs if they give a portion of their income back to his work.

Even so, God does expect us to be generous with our money. Let's take a look again at the words of Jesus in Matthew:

---

25. This quote is often attributed to Victor Hugo, Amy Carmichael, and Robert Louis Stevenson; however, its true origin seems to be unknown.

> Thus, when you give to the needy, sound no trumpet before you, as the hypocrites do in the synagogues and in the streets, that they may be praised by others. Truly, I say to you, they have received their reward. But when you give to the needy, do not let your left hand know what your right hand is doing, so that your giving may be in secret. And your Father who sees in secret will reward you.[26]

Notice that according to Jesus it's not a matter of if we give, but rather when we give. It is expected that we will.

Let's look at the Old Testament. The last book of the Old Testament is called Malachi, and he prophesied at a time when the Israelites' passion for God was waning. They had become disinterested in the God of their ancestors and, as a result, they began to, among other things, cheat God in their generosity and giving. Into all this, the voice of Malachi (serving as God's mouthpiece) surfaces to challenge their faithlessness. Look here:

> Will man rob God? Yet you are robbing me. But you say, "How have we robbed you?" In your tithes and contributions. You are cursed with a curse, for you are robbing me, the whole nation of you. Bring the full tithe into the storehouse, that there may be food in my house. And thereby put me to the test, says the Lord of hosts, if I will not open the windows of heaven for you and pour down for you a blessing until there is no more need.[27]

Consider for a moment the idea of "robbing God." My family lived in Northern California near the city of Stockton. At the time we moved there, Stockton was ranked among the top cities for vehicle theft. Sure enough, we had our vehicles broken into an average of once per year! I have some pastor friends who lived in the same area, and they had their house broken into in broad daylight. One day they came home to their house ransacked and emptied of all valuables—computers, musical instruments, even their Boston Terrier pup Frodo! Brutal.

26. Matt 6:2–4 (ESV).
27. Mal 3:8–10 (ESV).

Introducing Some Potential Next Steps

God confronts his people through the prophet Malachi and lets them know that what they're doing in holding back on their giving is actually an act of robbery against God. But notice in the challenge to return to faithfulness, God gives them a promise that if they'll do so, he would pour out blessings on them until all their needs were met.

How about one more example, just for good measure? The book of Proverbs has a way of speaking an entire novel in just a few sentences:

> Honor the LORD with your wealth and with the first of all your crops. Then your barns will be filled with plenty, and your vats will burst with wine.[28]

OK, with just a few verses I think we've established that God expects his people to be faithfully generous with their resources—especially money, but perhaps for reasons you may not expect. I want to offer you a few things to consider that I've learned over the years regarding financial generosity.

Consideration #1: God Owns It All.

In the book of Matthew, Jesus' disciples come to him and ask him this question: "Tell us, when will these things happen? What will be the sign of your coming and the end of the age?"[29]

They are curious about the end of all things. When will Jesus come back? What should we be looking for? Maybe you've wondered about some of the same things. Jesus decides to answer their questions in detail, but he takes a more indirect route. He decides to answer their questions in a series of what are called parables.

If you're unfamiliar with parables, they are essentially made-up stories. But, they are stories with intent and purpose. I've heard parables described as "made-up stories to make a point." In each of Jesus' parables, of which there are many, he is illustrating a point. Further, you'll notice as you study the parables of Jesus that they

---

28. Prov 3:9–10 (CEB).
29. Matt 24:3 (CEB)

are layered. In other words, Jesus has a way of making several points in a single story.

The gist of the overall answer Jesus gives to his disciples concerning the timing of his return at the end of all things is this: "No one knows the day or hour, so stay alert and be ready!"

However, there are more layers to consider and, in Matt 25:14–30, Jesus tells the story of a wealthy man who leaves to go on a long trip. Before he leaves, he calls together his servants and distributes his possessions to them in varying amounts with the expectation they will steward wisely what has been given to them. Here is how Jesus sets the story up:

> The kingdom of heaven is like a man who was leaving on a trip. He called his servants and handed his possessions over to them.[30]

If you're unfamiliar with the story, the short version is that he gave one servant five valuable coins, another two valuable coins, and another servant one valuable coin. The first two servants went to work leveraging the resources in business dealings and doubled the money, but the "one-talent" servant went and buried his valuable coin. After a long time, the master returns to settle accounts. The first two servants are commended and rewarded for their shrewd stewardship, but the last servant is condemned for his laziness and lack of stewardship.

Now, most Bible teachers (not all) would agree that the characters in Jesus' story translate this way: (a) the master is Jesus, (b) the servants are his followers (us!), and (c) the valuable coins represent all the gifts, talents, and resources God has given to us.

Further, they would generally agree that the main takeaways Jesus is trying to highlight with the story are (a) just like the servants didn't know the day or hour when their master would return asking for an accounting, neither do we know the day or hour of the return of our master, Jesus; (b) until Christ returns, we need to follow the example of the first two servants who invested and maximized what had been entrusted to them.

---

30. Matt 25:14 (CEB)

Introducing Some Potential Next Steps

All good so far? Let's look at another layer or two down. Notice that in Jesus' bid to communicate to his disciples the unpredictable timing of his return—and therefore the need to be ready—he also firmly establishes ownership. Who do the servants belong to? Who do all the resources belong to? All belong to Christ. Listen to how the apostle Paul addresses this:

> Don't you know that you have the Holy Spirit from God, and you don't belong to yourselves? You have been bought and paid for, so honor God with your body.[31]

Further, all we've been blessed with comes from God. Listen to King David from the Old Testament capture this idea of everything and everyone belonging to God:

> The earth is the LORD's and everything in it, the world and its inhabitants too.[32]

Friend, if we do not get the ownership issue right, we will never get the generosity issue right. If we continue to follow Jesus believing that we own everything, rather than believing God owns everything, we will have a difficult time giving to God what we believe is rightfully ours. However, if we settle in our hearts that God owns it all and has made us stewards of his resources, then it is far easier to give back to him what is his to begin with.

I encourage you to settle this in your heart—God owns it all.

Consideration #2: God Does Not Need Your Money.

I want to let this one sink in a bit. Read it again, God . . . does not . . . need . . . your money. What a ridiculous thought to begin with, right? God is somehow "broke" and "down on his luck" and needs us to bail him out?

First, we just established it's his anyway. Second, if this is true, then there must be another reason(s) why God would work so

---

31. 1 Cor 6:19(b)–20 (CEB).
32. Ps 24:1 (CEB).

diligently throughout Scripture to shape a heart of generosity in his children. And there is.

I picked up a phrase from a pastor a few years ago that has stuck with me, and I want to share it with you: God does not want something *from* you—he wants something *for* you.

Again, God has not hit a minimum balance in his bank account, and he's not in possession of a tin cup that he extends to his followers whenever they attend church. He is after something much more profound.

Remember when we addressed "The Goal" a few chapters back? God is conforming us into the likeness (image) of himself: of Jesus. Well, what does that image look like? There are many aspects, and we hit on some in that chapter, but let me give you another: irrational generosity.

God is the greatest giver! This is his image . . . who he is. Listen to this most famous of all verses in the Bible:

> God so loved the world that he gave his only Son, so that everyone who believes in him won't perish but will have eternal life.[33]

God didn't just give a little—he gave everything. It was irrational generosity toward humanity motivated by love. His goal is not your financial resources, but rather your conformation into Christ's image of generosity. And, at no other time do we look more like Jesus than when we're living generously.

Consideration #3: Giving of Our Hard-Earned Income Will Always Return Us to the Vital Issue of Trust in God.

In the Old Testament, we read of God rescuing the children of Israel out from under the brutal, iron fist of the Pharaohs. Some Bible scholars estimate he led over one million people out of Egypt through the leadership of Moses. As we read the journey of the children of Israel from slavery in Egypt to the promised land, we have to keep in mind that they had been enslaved for

---

33. John 3:16 (CEB).

Introducing Some Potential Next Steps

over four hundred years. Every aspect of their lives was monitored and controlled, from diet, to work, to rest, leisure, and more. For generations, they only knew one way of life, so God had to essentially forge an entirely new people group under his loving care and guidance.

Part of this forging was in the arena of trust. Will the children of Israel choose to trust God to lead them, provide for them, protect them, and keep his promises, instead of an Egyptian taskmaster? Spoiler alert: they didn't always choose so well in this department. In fact, on their worst days they begged to go back into Egyptian slavery! Interestingly, one of the ways he chose to do this was through their food intake.

Let's return to something we mentioned in chapter three regarding Exodus 16 and God's plan to provide food through quail at night and something called "manna" in the morning. The word "manna" essentially means "what?" or "what is it?" It was so named because when the children of Israel first saw it, they asked one another, "What is it?" (Side note, I can relate. I've cooked many a meal where I've been asked, "What is that?")

The Bible describes manna as this small, sweet wafer that appeared on the ground each morning via God's miraculous provision. Let's pause right there. What? No need to go out and hunt or fish, or call DoorDash—it just shows up in the form of sweet little breakfast cakes? That's an amazing deal!

He instructed the Israelites to gather only enough for their daily needs. And here is the moment of truth, right? Will God provide the next morning? Will he really provide food each day? In fact, Exod 16:4 tells us this was a bit of a test from God to see if the children of Israel would follow his instruction and trust him to provide.

Unfortunately, some of them did not fully trust in God's promise and decided to gather more manna than they needed, thinking it would be better to have extra just in case. However, when they tried to store the excess manna, it spoiled and became infested with maggots. Eventually, it seems, they got the point that

God could indeed be trusted to provide, and he did for forty years during their wandering in the wilderness.

Now, let's make the connection to us. Will we choose to trust in God to provide? Or will we instead hang on to what we have, and attempt to gather more? You see friends, God's expectation really is an invitation. An invitation to what? Trust.

Imagine with me that you've made the decision to give some of your income to your local church (more on this in a minute) to honor God and see the gospel message of his love reach further into your community to impact more people like it has you. Let's be honest, you can think of ten things—both needs and certainly wants—that the money could go to in your life! Honoring God with our wealth and the "first fruit" (Prov 3:9) of our income will always return us to this question, "Can I trust God to take care of my needs?" Another way: "Can I trust God to somehow resupply what now seems lacking in my monthly budget?"

This last question is a great segue to our next consideration. For now, I encourage you to settle in your heart that God is completely trustworthy as a provider.

Consideration #4: God Is a God of "Resupply."

One of my favorite stories in all of the Bible is found in 1 Kgs 17. It involves a rock-star prophet named Elijah, and a widow and her son from a town called Zarephath. Here is the set up: There is a drought in the land, and God speaks to Elijah and tells him to go to Zarephath because he has chosen a widow to provide for his needs. Elijah does what God says, shows up at the town gate, sees a woman collecting sticks, and calls out to her, "Please get a little water for me in this cup so I can drink" (verse 10). She does so, but Elijah doesn't stop there—he then asks for a piece of bread to which the woman responds:

Introducing Some Potential Next Steps

> "As surely as the Lord your God lives," she replied, "I don't have any food; only a handful of flour in a jar and a bit of oil in a bottle. Look at me. I'm collecting two sticks so that I can make some food for myself and my son. We'll eat the last of the food and then die."[34]

Her response snaps us right back to reality—there is a famine in the land; her husband is dead, leaving the woman and her son extremely vulnerable. The last thing she needs is another mouth to feed, especially when her and her son are on their last meal. Ever.

It's as if her response flies right over Elijah's head. Listen to what he says:

> "Don't be afraid! Go and do what you said. Only make a little loaf of bread for me first. Then bring it to me. You can make something for yourself and your son after that."[35]

Are you kidding me? Who does this? She and her son are going to die, and he is asking for their last meal! Perhaps someone needs to teach the prophet about empathy, or "doing unto others what you would have them do to you," or just basic manners. For heaven's sake, take a class in social awareness!

But, we have to read on to what he says next:

> "This is what Israel's God, the Lord, says: The jar of flour won't decrease and the bottle of oil won't run out until the day the Lord sends rain on the earth."[36]

In other words, "If you go make me some bread using up your last bit of oil and flour, it won't run dry because God will resupply both jars not just once, but over and over until this drought is over."

This is a moment of truth for this poor widow, isn't it? Will she choose the logical thing which would be to stretch the flour and oil for herself and her son at least one more day? Or would

---

34. 1 Kgs 17:12 (CEB).
35. 1 Kgs 17:13 (CEB).
36. 1 Kgs 17:14 (CEB).

she choose to trust that God would indeed resupply what she gives away? Let's find out:

> The widow went and did what Elijah said. So the widow, Elijah, and the widow's household ate for many days. The jar of flour didn't decrease nor did the bottle of oil run out, just as the LORD spoke through Elijah.[37]

My friend, God is a God of resupply. What he re-supplies may not look like what you expect, or come in the way you expect, or even the timing you expect. But he is faithful, trustworthy, and generous with his resupply.

Consideration #5: The System God Has Chosen to Provide for His Church and Kingdom[38] Is Through the Faithful Generosity of Those Who Have Chosen to Follow Him.

In chapter 2, we talked about the transcendence of God which includes his all-powerfulness. One of the things I've often pondered is why God, in his omnipotence (all-powerful), would leave the realm of something so critical—like meeting the financial needs of his church (his people)—to *people*? Why not just take this one on yourself? Why leave this all-important task to frail, faulty, forgetful, and sometimes greedy human beings?

And yet he does. What an honor, however, when you stop and think this through. God desires to partner with us to bless other people, care for others, encourage others, and provide for the needs of others. What an amazing honor and blessing to be included in such a crucial task! And he's promised to take care of us as we do. Pretty good deal if you ask me.

OK, you may now be asking: "What now? I understand God's expectation and why, and these considerations make some sense,

---

37. 1 Kings 17:15–16 (CEB).

38. "Theology. The eternal spiritual sovereignty of God or Christ, or the sphere over which this extends, in heaven or on earth; the spiritual state of which God is the head. Also: this state as the final abode of the redeemed after their life on earth." Oxford English Dictionary, "Kingdom."

Introducing Some Potential Next Steps

but what is my next step?" You'll notice the title of this chapter is "Introducing Some Potential Next Steps." I use the word "potential" because it would be awfully presumptuous of me to prescribe, in some one-size-fits-all box, the exact next step of faith for each person who reads this book—especially related to giving.

Instead, I offer you a simple framework for a potential next step I've offered to Christ-followers for a long time now. What you choose to do with this is between you and Jesus. It goes like this: give, give generously, give consistently. Let's take them briefly one at a time.

Give

Simply begin the spiritual practice of generosity. Often a helpful way to begin is through percentage giving. Keep in mind, this concept of percentage giving is not without its controversy and debate among pastors, churches, and theologians—sometimes referred to as the "tithing debate." The gist of the debate is whether tithing ("tithe" simply means "a tenth part") is a New Testament principle or not. Regardless which side of the debate one might land, all parties would agree that growing in generosity is crucial to growing in Jesus. My goal is not to enter that fray in this book, but rather to simply help you take your next step of faith.

So, let me hit on an aspect of percentage giving that I think all parties will agree on regardless of where they land in the debate—the beauty is that it makes it easier for all income levels to participate! If you can imagine three friends of varying income levels—one wealthy, one middle-class, and one earning a lower income—decide together they want to begin this journey of generosity and decide to give a certain percentage of their income, say 8 percent for our example (no real scriptural significance). By utilizing a percentage of income rather than a certain dollar amount, they all get to participate according to their means. The wealthy person gives 8 percent of a larger amount, and the lower-income earner gives 8 percent of a lesser amount.

I realize this may elicit more questions than answers, like "What percentage should I begin with?," "Would that be on the gross or net?," or "What if I can't afford even my current budget because of debt and some poor financial decisions?" All good questions, and all outside the goal and purview of this book. However, I would encourage you to schedule some time with your pastor or one of the leaders at your church to get your questions answered.

For now, I offer this simple, potential next step of faith: give. And consider starting with a percentage of your income. One final note here: I'm certain the question may be popping up in your mind by now, "Where should I give?" Great question. Ultimately, the Holy Spirit will guide you as you pray and ask him. Even so, I would encourage you to begin giving to the church you attend. We spent time a few pages back talking about the beautiful work the body of Christ (the church) does in each community around the world, and every local church depends on the faithful generosity of Christ-followers like you.

Give Generously

We talked a few pages back under Consideration #2 that contained within the image of God is irrational generosity. Jesus is the ultimate giver, even giving his life for humanity. This is the image we are being conformed into!

At one point in the apostle Paul's ministry, he worked with some of the churches he helped start, to collect an offering for the beleaguered Christians in Jerusalem facing famine and poverty at the time. In his second letter to the Christians at Corinth, he wrote:

> What I mean is this: the one who sows a small number of seeds will also reap a small crop, and the one who sows a generous amount of seeds will also reap a generous crop.[39]

Jesus also taught using imagery of sowing and reaping, I think because there are some powerful lessons the process can teach us.

---

39. 2 Cor 9:6 (CEB).

Introducing Some Potential Next Steps

First, we reap what we sow. If we plant tomato seeds in the ground, we receive tomatoes back. Second, the scale we receive back is often not proportionate to what we plant—it's far more. We don't just receive one tomato from one seed—we receive a crop of them! We could say it like this: we receive an increased return. Third, we must wait to receive our crop. The tomatoes don't just spring up immediately. We might say it like this: sowing and reaping is the process of delayed gratification.

Paul seems to be hitting on this second reality of nature: increased return. Knowing that his first-century, largely agrarian readers would understand this, he encourages them not to sow sparingly, but rather to sow generously. Why? Because he desires something for them: a large harvest!

I have a friend who is a financial advisor and he and his wife give nearly 50 percent of their income away! I know other Christ-followers who increase their giving by 1 percent each year with the eventual goal of giving away more than what they live on. In fact, I know of a pastor who has reached the point over time where he and his wife now give away 90 percent of their income and live on 10 percent!

Am I suggesting this needs to be you? No. What I am suggesting is that you spend some time praying and ask God to help you and show you how to sow generously just like he does. What you'll find is this beautiful reciprocity: you'll enjoy the benefit of reaping generously. Sowing generosity, reaping generosity. This is not why we give; it's simply a by-product of sowing and reaping.

One last note here: when we sow something physical (money) into something spiritual (God and his work), we often enjoy a spiritual harvest. I think you'll be blown away by all the ways God surprises you, encourages you, and blesses you as you trust him with your finances.

Weight Shift

Give Consistently

Finally, my friend, as you engage this spiritual practice of trusting God with your finances and mirroring him in generosity, I encourage you to do so consistently. Make it a practice.

I have found many reasons why some folks start their journey of generosity well, only to fall into a pattern of fits and starts along the way. Perhaps some fall on hard times financially, some get disappointed in waiting for the delayed harvest, and sometimes folks just get out of rhythm and practice, to name a few. Regardless, the principles of steadfastness, faithfulness, perseverance, and consistency as we follow Christ is woven in spades throughout Scripture. Again, our leader in all this is Christ himself. Look here from the writer of Hebrews:

> Appreciate your pastoral leaders who gave you the Word of God. Take a good look at the way they live, and let their faithfulness instruct you, as well as their truthfulness. There should be a consistency that runs through us all. For Jesus doesn't change—yesterday, today, tomorrow—he's always totally himself.[40]

And from the psalmist:

> But the LORD's plan stands forever; / what he intends to do lasts from one generation to the next.[41]

Friend, when we consistently trust God with our finances, we build a personal history of God's consistent faithfulness toward us. I've discovered over time and growth in my own journey with Jesus in this area that he is totally, completely trustworthy.

So, I encourage you to trust God with your resources and begin to give, give generously, and give consistently.

---

40. Heb 13:7–8 (MSG).
41. Ps 33:11 (CEB).

Introducing Some Potential Next Steps

CHAPTER 6 DISCUSSION QUESTIONS:

1. Which one(s) of these six potential next steps seems to be the area the Holy Spirit may be guiding you to engage?
2. When you think about praying, what comes to mind? Was this chapter helpful to you? How so?
3. Is it easy for you to serve others, or difficult? Why?
4. When you think about consistently giving back to God a portion of your income, what types of feelings and thoughts come up?

Conclusion

I WANT TO END the way we began, with the idea of shifting your weight and taking your next step of faith. While writing this book, I became curious about the science of walking, from how infants learn to walk, to various muscle groups involved, and what happens in the brain.

Essentially, each step we take is a controlled fall. We purposefully lean our bodies off-balance, then extend our leg to catch our "fall," regain balance, then wash, rinse, and repeat. This is how babies learn to walk, and frankly why there is often more falling initially than walking. However, as we grow, the process of our controlled falling eventually becomes less dangerous, and more durable, even second nature.

Our high-wire artist, Philippe, had to make the choice whether he would keep his right leg anchored to the flank of the building, or shift his weight into a controlled fall (a potentially very long fall). You too have a decision to make regarding your next steps along the high wire of faith, but unlike Philippe, your trust is not in your own skill, or fickle weather patterns, or the integrity of the cable anchors—yours is in Christ who will never leave you or forsake you (Heb 13:5), who is faithful and true (Rev 19:11), who created you (Ps 139), and loves you (1 John 3:1).

My prayer is that you will choose to shift your weight . . . again.

Appendix

WHAT FOLLOWS ARE SOME resources I've found helpful as I engage the Bible, and as of the writing of this book each of these are available for free (except for the Lectio Divina Journal). Keep in mind this list will likely change within a few short years as technology advances, new ideas are born, and new companies come online. Further, this is nowhere near a comprehensive list. I've purposefully left it short because I'm certain the pastors and leaders of the local church you attend will have additional resources to recommend.

1. Blue Letter Bible: This is a wonderful tool for Bible study. It has an array of tools including an advanced search function that allows you to search for specific books of the Bible, phrases, words, and even partial words. You are able to compare various translation of the Bible side by side, pull up maps and timelines, and even engage in some advanced study of words in the original language if you want. Website: https://www.blueletterbible.org

2. Daily Audio Bible: A way to listen to the Bible each day, as the host reads from a different version of the Bible each week. There are options to listen to the entire Bible through in one year, listen only to the proverbs of the day, and even a Daily Audio Bible Kids option. Website: https://dailyaudiobible.com

Appendix

3. Lectio Divina Journal: "Lectio Divina" is Latin for "Divine Reading" and is a way to thoughtfully and prayerfully engage Scripture. This method of engaging the Bible has been part of Christian tradition since the earliest centuries of the church. A pastor friend of mine named Greg Russinger developed a journal to guide people through the simple, powerful process. Website: https://www.lectiodivinajournal.com

4. YouVersion: This application puts the Bible in digital form into your hands for free. You can select any portion of the Bible you want to read, as well as select from a long list of various translations depending on which version you want to read. Further, they have a link to a robust library of Bible reading plans and daily devotionals. Website: https://www.bible.com

Bibliography

Athanasius. "Athanasian Creed." Christian Reformed Church. https://www.crcna.org/welcome/beliefs/creeds/athanasian-creed.
Bilezikian, Gilbert. *Christianity 101*. Grand Rapids: Zondervan, 1993.
Clark, Mark. *The Problem of God: Answering a Skeptics's Challenges to Christianity*. Grand Rapids: Zondervan, 2017.
Gumbel, Nicky. *Questions for Life: A Practical Introduction to the Christian Faith*. Nashville: W Publishing Group, 2016.
Josephus, Flavius. *The Antiquity of the Jews*. Translated by William Whiston. Ebook. https://www.gutenberg.org/files/2848/2848-h/2848-h.htm#link18noteref-9.
Keller, Timothy. "The Gospel in All Its Forms." Christianity Today, May 2008. https://www.christianitytoday.com/2008/05/gospel-in-all-its-forms/.
———. *The Reason for God: Belief in an Age of Skepticism*. New York: Penguin, 2009.
Lewis, C. S. *The Four Loves*. New York: HarperCollins, 2002.
McDowell, Josh. *Evidence that Demands a Verdict: Historical Evidences for the Christian Faith*. 1st ed. San Bernardino: Campus Crusade for Christ, 1972.
McDowell, Josh, and Sean McDowell. *Evidence that Demands a Verdict: Life-Changing Truth for a Skeptical World*. 4th ed. Nashville: Thomas Nelson, 2017.
McGrath, Alister. *Christian Theology: An Introduction*. West Sussex: Wiley Blackwell, 2017.
McKnight, Scot. *The King Jesus Gospel: The Original Good News Revisited* Grand Rapids: Zondervan, 2016.
Mulholland, M. Robert Jr. *Invitation to a Journey: A Road Map for Spiritual Formation*. Downer's Grove, IL: InterVarsity, 1993.
Ortberg, John. *Who Is This Man?: The Unpredictable Impact of the Inescapable Jesus*. Grand Rapids: Zondervan, 2012.
Oxford English Dictionary. "Evangelical." https://www.oed.com/dictionary/evangelical_adj?tab=meaning_and_use.
———. "Idiom." https://www.oed.com/dictionary/idiom_n?tab=meaning_and_use#909611.
———. "Immanent." https://www.oed.com/dictionary/immanent_adj?tab=meaning_and_use#995598.

Bibliography

———. "Incarnation." https://www.oed.com/dictionary/incarnation_n?tab=meaning_and_use#769378.

———. "Kingdom." https://www.oed.com/dictionary/kingdom_n?tab=meaning_and_use#40198535.

———. "Messiah." https://www.oed.com/dictionary/messiah_n?tab=meaning_and_use&tl=true#37405064.

———. "Prophesy." https://www.oed.com/dictionary/prophesy_v?tab=meaning_and_use#28236613.

———. "Transcendent." https://www.oed.com/dictionary/transcendent_adj?tab=meaning_and_use&tl=true.

Petit, Philippe. "Philippe Petit: The Journey Across the High Wire." TED, March 2012. https://www.ted.com/talks/philippe_petit_the_journey_across_the_high_wire?language=en.

Spurgeon, Charles. "The Birth of Christ." The Spurgeon Center, December 24, 1854. https://www.spurgeon.org/resource-library/sermons/the-birth-of-christ/#flipbook/.

StepBible.org. "1 Thessalonians 5." https://www.stepbible.org/?q=version=ESV@reference=1Thess.5&options=NVHUG.

Stewart, Don. "What Are the Major Theories of Bible Translation? (Formal Equivalence and Dynamic Equivalence)." Blue Letter Bible. https://www.blueletterbible.org/Comm/stewart_don/faq/bible-translations/question7-major-theories-of-bible-translation.cfm.

Stott, John. *Basic Christianity*. Grand Rapids: Eerdmans, 2008.

Tacitus, Publius Cornelius. *The Annals of Tacitus*. University of Chicago, July 12, 2024. https://penelope.uchicago.edu/Thayer/E/Roman/Texts/Tacitus/Annals/15B*.html.

Tozer, A. W. *The Knowledge of the Holy*. New York: HarperCollins, 1961.

Wright, N. T. *Simply Jesus: A New Vision of Who He Was, What He Did, and Why He Matters*. New York: HarperCollins, 2011.

www.ingramcontent.com/pod-product-compliance
Lightning Source LLC
Chambersburg PA
CBHW072158100426
42738CB00011BA/2463